THE SONNETS

THE SONNETS

TRANSLATING AND REWRITING SHAKESPEARE

EDITED BY

Sharmila Cohen and Paul Legault

TELEPHONE BOOKS

BROOKLYN, NEW YORK

Contents

Introduction

Shakespeare's sonnets were first made available in their entirety through piracy: the cover image of this collection comes from the first printing of the collected work, which was published by T.T. (Thomas Thorpe) in 1609 without authorization. In the next printed version, which appeared in 1640, the sonnets were rearranged to alter the themes of the work. These thefts provided the original resources for the sonnets and fit nicely within the Shakespearean tradition: we all want to inhabit his texts, put our mark on them, break them down, steal from them.

In this anthology, Telephone's first full-length book, we have invited 160 poets to each *translate* one sonnet from English to English. Of course, we are aware of the many translations of Shakespeare's works into modern English, such as the ones designed to help students better understand the content beyond the sometimes challenging and antiquated language. We also want to offer a new and contemporary understanding of Shakespeare, but something beyond that of simply breaking through the boundaries of an ever-changing lexicon—our hope was that the contributors would approach the original texts from their multitude of vantage points, that they would board the ship, loot and pillage, break things down, and reconstruct it all in a fashion that would allow us to view multiple dimensions of the original work in a new light, as a new structure.

The poets gave us exactly what we were looking for: in this collection you will find translations ranging from images to theoretical discussions to numerical equations and beyond. If Shakespeare's framework was the sonnet, then our contributors' framework was Shakespeare.

As the Bard says in Sonnet 55:

> Not marble, nor the gilded monuments
> Of princes, shall outlive this powerful rhyme

Or as Geoffrey G. O'Brien interprets it:

> The sonnet will admit it needs to live,
> A contradiction ending won't forgive

Shakespeare's sonnets live on, even beyond their original order and content and form—we hope that this collection exists as a part of that life.

—S. C. & P. L.

THE
SONNETS

Steve McCaffery

SONNET 1

Two Alternative Translations of Shakespeare's Sonnet 1: 'From fairest creatures we desire increase'

a.i.o.ua.eo.a.u.a	((((((((((
a.eo.o.a.ao.o.u.e	))))))))))
e.a.o.a.a.ao.a	((((((((((
ei.aoe.a.e.oae	))))))))))
e.ue.eaa.a.e.u	((((((((((
o.ae.e.o.a.o.ue.a	)))))))))))
a.u.i.ea.ia.a.ae.u	((((((((((
e.o.a.e.a.oea.o.a.ea	)))))))))))
a.o.a.ao.o.u.ui.o	((((((((((
a.aa.a.oa.oi.a.aea	))))))))))
a.u.i.ai.ea.a.e.o	(((((((((((
i.a.eaa.a.u.a.a.a	))))))))))
a.u.i.o.o.u.o.oa.a	))((((((((((
	(())))))))()

from "TRG Research Report 1: Translation" in *Open Letter*, second series, no. 4 (spring 1973).

Jen Bervin

SONNET 2

2

When forty winters shall beseige thy brow,
And dig deep trenches in thy beauty's field,
Thy youth's proud livery, so gazed on now,
Will be **a** tattered **weed, of small worth** held:
Then being **asked** where all thy beauty lies,
Where all the treasure of thy lusty days,
To say, within thine own deep-sunken eyes,
Were an all-eating shame and thriftless praise.
How much more praise deserved thy beauty's use,
If thou couldst answer 'This fair child of mine
Shall sum my count and make my old excuse,'
Proving his beauty by succession thine,
  This were **to be new made** when thou art old,
  And see thy blood warm when thou feel'st it cold.

from *Nets* (Ugly Duckling Presse, 2004)

Rae Armantrout

SONNET 3

Your dad told me to tell you
how good you look to him right now.
Check yourself out. (I'm sure you do.)
You're a very pretty boy.
But the thing is, that won't last
Have you ever seen a pert old man?
An insouciant septuagenarian?
I thought not. They're invisible.
And you'll be invisible too!
What will your dad have
to look at then? Do you think growth
rebounds each year? Wrong!
It has to be outsourced. Sublet.
Get with the program.
Your dad will be watching.

Dana Ward

Cinq Saveurs: A Children's Book

—for Dodie Bellamy

"I did spend one lovely evening with John Wieners, with Kevin and Raymond Foye. We went to dinner and out for drinks at Tosca Cafe in North Beach. Afterwards, Wieners asked us if we'd like some digestive aids, and he went into a corner store in Chinatown and bought us each a pack of Lifesavers. I keep that pack of Lifesavers in a drawer in my desk."

What would I do with those candies if I had them? Save them forever, an heirloom I'd guard with my life to be given not even to Viv but somehow just given away. For the moment I guess that's impossible here. There are too many Charons between us for gifts to bridge the rough abyss they shelter & reveal. Shatter & confirm. It's so cherry though, thinking economy's grave, with no warm boughs fanned out above the absence of its marker, & no way to pay your respects.

The morning I read Dodie's post I knew I'd be nourished by its questions forever. The question of the lineage of love's exilic candy, the question of eternal indigestion, & infinite wishing & infinite money, of preservation, consumption, & hunger & care, of the amulet imbued with the terrifying angel of its truth which appears when you eat it.

I know their magic would seduce me in the end. I'd succumb because it's what I always do. I'm prone to heartburn at night & can totally see myself sneaking downstairs, pacing in front of the drawer where they're kept, giving in, nursing one for hours in bed to at least maybe savor this rare treasure I'd be killing. A saturate lemony balm would fill my chest, a kind of opiated Pledge of vapor sugar. I'd wake up in a beachfront chimeric hotel. There, I would be freshly svelte & snort pills, contented by the beauty of the sea.

Beautiful. Beautiful beautiful. God. I use that word, 'beautiful', loosely, like fuck. Fuck beauty. Beauty fuck. Infinite too. I throw them around nouveau riche & incautious for the sake of crucial atmospheres invoked by their abuse; melancholic volubility of waste & exhaustion, long decimated vertical intransigence of god. I guess I think my body is a wishing well somehow? I felt weirdly lonely last year.

The emptiness in me was suddenly filled picking Julian up from the airport. I drove there through one of those furious snows that doesn't in the end amount to much. Part of the drive I made blind, or nearly so. By the time I found J all the squalling had stopped, & the sky was like soft-core apocalypse kitsch; cloudbanks split open by sunbursts, enormous beams broken in petaling strobes.

Driving home I explained my whole Life Saver thing. I had an idea about trying to heal. We'd buy our own roll, go down to the river, make wishes, & throw them all in. I wanted this placebo spell to satisfy my hunger for the real ones safely kept in Dodie's desk. The bad karma of wishing they were mine & the facile hunger for miracle cures.

There's a mall, & it's sort of like a fortress they've built on the floodwall that grades along the river. We stopped by their candy store to hook up our supplies. They didn't stock the old Life Saver rolls, just those gummi kind that come in little bags. I decided those would have to do. Maybe they'd finally be better. In trying to excise a fantasy why not begin by unmaking its fidelity, first to itself, & then to every other thing.

We walked out along the footbridge that spans the Ohio. Our river, all aureate green & shit brown, is just a blemish that's subsumed platonic water. I launched a few over then Julian did. I saved the last two, & we stood in the spot equidistant from Kentucky & Ohio. We counted to three, & threw them in. I imagined we were plucking the very last petals from the very last Calvinist TULIP. He loves me. & he loves me not.

I asked Julian if xe'd wished for anything & xe said xe hadn't. I said I'd forgotten as well. We wondered if the bridge had enough elevation to allow someone to kill themself, despairing. We talked it over but we figured you'd survive. Hypothermia maybe. Broken limbs. & of course, in the end, you might drown. But the impact wouldn't be the thing that did it. Julian pointed to the banks of the river & talked about a murder ballad set along the water. I think xe knows how to play it on guitar.

I had meant to wish for the ruin of despair, for its destruction, or for it to be changed into something really awesome, like Los Angeles maybe, or a kitten. I guess that's like asking for infinite wishes, when the genie turns its gaze from your face but says yes.

We walked back to the car in the cold & I had these Sunflower Sutra sort of feelings. I hadn't been this happy in awhile. On our way home we stopped for beer & I asked Julian before xe ran into the store to grab a roll of Life Savers I could keep as an emblem of our weekend. The package had the French & English both. Cinq Savuers. I savored the word in my mouth.

When the baby was born I felt money. I wanted her to never have to suffer so I started wanting whatever there was—an 'instinctual' hunger for a barrier of wealth to build around her body like a dreamland. That this terror came on me like an angel from without means only it was shot through my body already, waiting to be called to work by love. From the floor of the well at St Anne's to the Upwey to the fountain in the trees at St. Melar's, to the Trevi with its winged & marble horses & its gods, its water made undrinkable through years of ceaseless wishing, in the winter like Christmas on Ice, braided rainbows in the summer the desire to be instantly & totally transformed has always been the sunshine of my life.

When David said "money is a negative eucharist" I can tell you that he wasn't really guessing. When people say "You need to get serious about your life now" they're not fucking with you. In the end though all they mean by that is money.

I put the Life Savers Julian bought in my drawer like that sonnet where nothing's inside. Pencils. Scotch Tape. A dead flip phone & jewel case. Envelopes, kept for addresses scrawled out in the wandering hand of a friend. A USB cable. Some book I've not read. Aspirin Thom bought for our hangovers. Resin, dark black, in a colorful bowl. A copy of the Cincinnati Kid that Nat left. A few flecks of glitter, paper specks, indeterminate dirt, & some pennies in the belly of the sun.

Paul Hoover

SONNET 5

Figure and Ground

If you must make a picture, paint within the frame.
Our gaze within two perfect eyes must dwell,
one blue, one brown, but otherwise the same.
It's only fair that one sight the other must excel;
such restless vision leads infinity on
to hideous zero, and confounds it there.
Pat Schrödinger's cat, image almost gone.
Overgrown, too slow, it has no where
nor here, nor angle of repose, and all that's left
is a pair of liquid scissors, paper thin glass,
beauty's final gesture, its metaphors bereft.
Neither it, nor I, remembers what an image was:
in a grandstand of mirrors, eyes multiplied meet
in one of light's car crashes, short but sweet.

CAConrad

(Soma)tic Poetry Exercise and resulting sonnet translation

QUARTZ CRYSTAL SHAKESPEARE SONNET TRANSLATION

—for Paul Legault & Sharmila Cohen

Piezoelectricity has proven the capacity quartz crystal has as a battery for electrical charge as well as its ability to store and transmit information. Let's take it a step further, a step FORWARD! Purchase a small clear quartz crystal. Set it in a bowl of salt over night to clean it. When you wake, flush the salt down the toilet, rinse your quartz, and DON'T LET ANYONE put their hands on it from now on. It's YOUR crystal, don't even let them SEE IT!

Choose one of Mr. Shakespeare's sonnets for an English-to-English translation, or have someone choose one for you. Paul Legault and Sharmila Cohen chose sonnet #6 for me. I translated two lines a day for seven days by holding my crystal to my mouth like a walky-talky to whisper the lines, SHOUT THE LINES. Several times every hour I STOPPED, held my crystal to my mouth and spoke into it, "Then let not winter's ragged hand deface / In thee thy summer, ere thou be distill'd:" JUST LIKE THAT! Tell your crystal the lines over and over throughout the day. "THEN LET NOT WINTER'S RAGGED HAND DEFACE / IN THEE THY SUMMER, ERE THOU BE DISTILL'D:" Years ago in a dream I found an enormous cluster of crystals emerging from a forest floor. A voice whispered to me, "Crystals are the bones of the Earth." I talk to our planet's crystal bones! So can you!

At night I instructed the crystal to PLEASE translate the lines for me in a dream. Programming our crystals is our right as citizens of the Milky Way, but they respond best with PLEASE and THANK YOU! In the morning, before rising, I placed my crystal on my forehead and meditated for a few minutes, lying quite still. Then I picked up pen and paper and wrote the first two lines that came to mind. Then I thanked the crystal, and started over with the next two lines.

TELL US WHEN SOMETHING IS HAPPENING OR WE MIGHT NOT KNOW

calories of mink dust and champagne
my gay minstrel show grows dark and bloody
too bad I left the lion-taming chair at home
my hope you fly through the door
my hope you fly through the window
we need you WHERE HAVE YOU GONE?
but for the sex good enough for poetry
love not me but the rind falling from my mouth
cradle of injury winging past the hearth
emancipate one tired shard by dawn
lumber is a tree
pork chop is a pig
is mean
is mean

Jeff Nagy — SONNET 7

CHORINHO 7 / ZERO À ESQUERDA

His head was like a robin's egg his tongue was like a safe
His chest was made of Adderall his heart was made of crepe

Do you think I like having to stand up here reminding you to have your pet spayed or neutered?
The sun and the moon are both born from the Bodhisattva's eyes. The *Sonnenstein*
Where hope to GOD my solar anus beamed / and forehead still burned with his kiss became a death camp.
Where 15,000 persons "pleated" in a public transparency rosy-fingered with perversions behind
The single eaglet of the d'Este at two, and at three. What is called BROWNING. What is.
What is called bergamot no purgative surfaced. This is the poem, the best source for *le succube verdâtre*
Et le rose lutin, as the turtle to her make, or not that nor 7 train. 61st woodside to Times Sq—m4m—24 (7train)"

< & >

And I smirked, having had her never having abased myself that way. How SHE LEAPT
And how, modestly, then, she slept, wearing the hijab of her dreams. A set-season aside
From the others, like a rib from which subducted springs a fifth, estate unto themselves. CHORINHO

Because poetry is not a TOY FOR CHILDREN or the positional grin last seen you
Wet ON MY MOUTH, a glue-gun wanting to be clean and out in the plotted
    day. I clapped
My hand across it and I kissed the hand

and then I remembered that I could speak to you, to
You, my love. And just as importantly I
Remembered that I could always choose not to.
Like, CHORINHO for let the hand speak,
For "for all the reasons" I will cease to be / a poet,

« À ne surprendre que naïvement d'accord. »

And the prow attended of dolphins I have a use for. CHORINHO: "That is one
    fucking car
And you are SO SO cute, beating around the beating around the bush."

Eugene Ostashevsky

SONNET 8

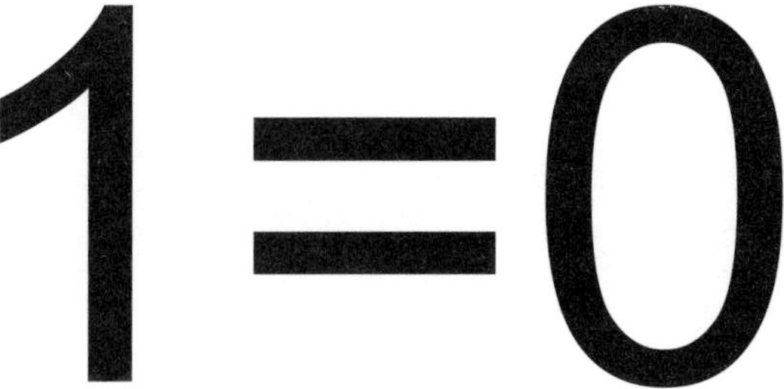

Once again the most general point is that symbols occur in sets and that the meaning of particular symbols is to be found in the contrast with other symbols rather than in the symbol as such.

Rachel Blau DuPlessis

SONNET 9

Trans-literalization of Sonnet 9 into a 28-line Dialogue

A. What is your issue with this?

B. I think it's ridiculous not to want children.
Aren't you in a committed-enough relationship?
Don't you want a picture of yourself being cute
the way you were. Etc. Like when you were four.

A. Do you really think this way—my "baby image in a baby,"
fair youth in youth? Does time just duplicate the static same?

B. But what are we here for? Forensics of the sonnet.
Be fruitful, multiply—it's another line of argument.

A. Your praise of me is complimentary manipulation.
Who's "having" this beautiful child anyway—maybe it will look
more like her! Plus who will raise said kid? Me tied down?
Or there's so much fresh widow, you've jumped track
from impregnation to my disappearance and her lack.

B. Really, don't you want to raise up some kind of image of yourself?
When this kid looks like you—it's like the future will be seeing you.

A. That amount of control over the future is a narcissistic fantasy.
I've seen them turn out badly—they aren't like their parents.
Things happen, losses are sustained, or, even accepting
the obsessive biology of your argument, by some twist of fate
a child might *look* like me but have the personality
of that depressive grandmother of mine. Why impregnate?

B. It's a suicide of beauty—I can't believe the rampant
spermy waste. You are so profligate, yet leave no stamp.
You love yourself too much; a future is for you, illusion.

A. What I love to do, I love to do, and what I don't, I don't.
Whom I do it with is not your care, and where you will, I won't.
You love your metaphors too much; that's the real delusion.

Tan Lin

SONNET 10

Oh no.
Unlucky.
OK
OK
OK Don't
You know
The roof's a mess. The future:
fix and fix.
What is gentle and unloved
loved a gentler way
to kindness.
Be someone and that someone be
Be someone else for me.

Hank Lazer

Shakenet Sonneleven

As fast in one and thou herein without if all
And let those harsh look which she carved thou
As those of thine that fresh mayest lives this folly were
Threescore years whom featureless when she bounteous thee shouldst
Print more for her seal gift she best and nature would
So age beauty when youngly which shalt wane
As fast thine blood when wisdom this were minded so.

Thou shalt from that which thou from youth
Increase cold decay the times would make the world away
Nature hath barrenly perish in bounty cherish
This folly age she gave thee more not made for store
Youngly those that fresh blood and made endowed
Meant thereby featureless wisdom thou shouldst print more:
If all were minded so, let that copy die.

Daniel Borzutzky SONNET 12

Market Ideology

When I do not count the clock that tells the time
and think of rodents in the mashed potatoes at Roosevelt High,
when Molotov cocktails explode in violins
and Choriomeningitis grows in hamster droppings,
when acid drips on perinea and coccyges
and cyanide is discovered in boxes of juice
and when the perfect sleeves of technocrats
sway forces beyond the control of the market,
I will dream this night
of the sorrows of your changing face
as you monitor the oscillations
of the turbulent Tokyo Stock Exchange.

When I do not count the clock that tells the time,
and stare instead at the perfect imperfection of the sea
which washes transparent horses to the shore
whose glittering intestines remind me
of my inability to outwit
the numinous logic of late capitalism,
I will not misread this vision
as a sign that my dividends will bust
but I will dream this night of shepherds and artichokes
and think of my portfolio
(a firm and salty bottom)
as I ejaculate on my financial forecast
for the following fiscal year.

Julian Talamantez Brolaski SONNET 13

sonnet 13 redux / the fair youth's response to the argument that he should breed

O cease your discourse on this mortal rot
So steeped in rank tautology that I
Against your nevercoming end begot
A creature with webbed feet and avian eye
Which for its outcase part keeps sullen pace
Makes no remark, beats itself for fury
And rakes its nails across that selfsame face
Engendered by your sweet philosophy.
So fill me not your husbandry withal—
Am I not yet your own embalmèd mate?
Has not my cup been overwhelmed with will?
& still your lust for increase will not slake?
Go lonely hence in woolen widow's weeds
I'll no more house the coffer for your greeds.

Matthew Rohrer

SONNET 14

Astrology is bullshit. Those
who think it tells them anything
about themselves or what kind
of mood everyone is going
to be in when one of the planets
does something
are idiots.
The stars don't care
who is elected. And the stars
don't know how beautiful
you are, almost too beautiful
to be true
or mine
Where are you? I go to bed
and hear that awful Eagles' song
in my head
YOU CAN'T HIDE YOUR LYIN' EYES

Prageeta Sharma

SONNET 15

Marjorie Welish's Vocabularies Sonnet

When I consider Patina correlated to pattern
holds mark overlapping mention simulating much. You said
that this huge stage is not art despite much mention,
suffering simulating abrasion/of canvas—no—business end.

When I perceive the sense of "belonging," a rake raking
gravel, a gravelly race her precursors never knew
vaunt in their youthful sap, you said paraphrase, speaking
at cross-purposes to abrasion, through use

And wear their brave state out of memory your receipt
had been utilized as that rake incarnate changing the subject
and the noise is kept alive, then the conceit
where wasteful time debateth with decay, I engraft

through the tatteredness of mass and time
that the noise is kept alive.

Astrid Lorange

SONNET 16

Vegetable, animal, soldier's pocket

The Walls Do Not Fall it gives off fragrance

of phosphorus at sunset the heaviest

taxpayer your idea of a rock ridge

climbs like an ibex and pawing orchids

artificial little jars of that garden:

garden facing three ways two points of Chuck

(who was against marriage?) queer like engines

transposed heads time of far planets budding

lost the ground in Eros particular

driven up the land the young man blacks out

He's in his father-critic sea-vest sweets

recalling it his oceanic life

recalling it his fingers text message

Timothy Liu & Jimmie Cumbie SONNET 17

Who to believe: one who goes or does not come?
If I were to say, it'd be about the way you left those lunar deserts,
though there are footfalls in the dust of some celestial tomb
which we'll never see from the window of our SUV and its reconditioned parts.
If I were a moth in your headlights, my compound eyes
and tan wings bursting into the beam would splay the night as roadkill graces
the pavement down the whole county wide where a convoy of rusted axles lies—
such a crashed heaven of creosote, an oil-soaked crustaceous ooze that defaces
so much more than a smear on the windshield, post midnight's persiflage.
Be comforted. We mean more than finger and tongue
and mouth and neck to a widower's rage.
And that pair of taillights pulsing into the bend becomes our song.
But were we children once more, immune to time,
you would rest your head in my lap and admit no crime.

18 THURSDAY, MARCH 3,2011

SHALL I compare thee
Thou art more lovely
Rough winds do shake the
And summer's leas hath
Sometime too hot **opters Kill 9 Afgi**
i wanted often is his go
so what every fair from fal
can you/ do ance, or nature's c
nothing
what a stupid eternal summe
cliche i
possession of
wanted all death brag
to feel It
anyway or n in eternal lines t(
remember) long as men can
it baby o long lives this and
remember
my name

"We were almost done collecting the wood when suddenly we saw the helicopters come," said Hemad, who, like many Afghans, has only one name. "There were two of them. The helicopters hovered over us, scanned us and we saw a green flash from the helicopters. Then they flew back high up, and in a second round they hovered over us and started shooting. They fired a rocket which landed on a tree. The tree branches fell over me, and shrapnel hit y right hand and my side."

'The tree, Hemad said, saved hIS life by concealing him from the helicopters, which, he said, "shot the boys one after another."

General Petraeus pledged to investigate. "We are deeply sorry for this tragedy an ... to h ... of

4 summer's: *Sommers*
7 sometime: *some-time*
9 summer: *Sommer*
11 wander'st: *wandr'st*

Rodrigo Toscano

SONNET 19

There's a decay rate for life, for which I see
That one upon the other all lives bleed.
I say let the effects of this rate run free,
Let all sorry suspensions of it breed,
For no sooner does it crap out hard and fast
All alibis for it, crooning, crashing—
But that's where to clip it—to make it last,
You gotta let sexy go on flaunting.
Let flow be slow as long as flow means grow;
Don't groove on a vibe that's just meant to grate.
When the cards are down, no one wants to throw
Life's potential into a poem like bait.
And check this: no matter what "scenes" may say,
This old sonnet still rocks from day to day.

Vanessa Place

SONNET 20

Boycott

A man's face with nature's own hand painted,
Hast thou, the master mister of my passion;
A man's gentle heart, but not acquainted
With shifting change, as is false men's fashion:
An eye more bright than theirs, less false in rolling,
Gilding the object whereupon it gazeth;
A man in hue all hues in his controlling,
Which steals men's eyes and men's souls amazeth.
And for a man wert thou first created;
Till Nature, as he wrought thee, fell a-doting,
And by addition me of thee defeated,
By adding one thing to my purpose nothing.
But since he prick'd thee out for men's pleasure,
Mine be thy love and thy love's use their treasure.

Norma Cole

Macaroni XXI

Also n'est-ce pas check it out como con el Muse
Clapping hands to the tinta des beaux vers,
Qui der Himmel selbst adorna
Et chaque beauté avec sa blonde proba,
S'approchant un paragone suberbo
Mit die Sonne e la luna, mit die Erde und les trésors de la thalassa,
And my mother (enormous laugh) ando perdido,
Que l'air céleste dans cet enorme colador stringa.
Hell yes! A me veramente amoureux ma veramente apunta,
Und so, croix-moi, me amor è si beau
Que n'importe quel enfant de madre benchè nicht so hell
Que ses chandelles enorme fixés en aire divino:
Parlino parlando plusqu'aiment bien ouï-dire;
Io non lodo ce but de non vender.

Ron Padgett

SONNET 22

My lass shall not dissuade me. I am bold.
Searing thy heart, which I will leap so airy,
Unhooked for joy in that I bonus must,
And in their shelves their hide lies buried dead.

And rig "pill" benches in thy sooty shield
Is but the beaming raiment of my art,
My hand folded and put away like combed hair
Turf, flying to us in the Dream Monsoons.

Who will reek of us when we are gone?
How lunch stores raze and splurge thy loot his muse
Where I may snot deluge nor be unglued:
How can I then be colder than thy wart?

My lass shall not dissuade me, though I fold
And peel and dry the sooty raiment of my hair.

(1963)

Laura Solomon

23 lines for white walls & dark rooms

for so long
in my hand
I held
my lover's

cock like an oar

little wonder now
how weirdly I steer

naked were the nudes...

over this get
can I not?

through imperfection's scenic park

slowly an actor forgets
everything
& is

the total eloquence of the universe expressed

long chemical moments...

the sun thickens, the wind slaps a tree

o green apple
of fury

when I touch you
I am fearless

does that
frighten you too?

Lonely Christopher

SONNET 24

I found you there in my parents' backyard
You were just looking right into the sun
I told you quit acting like some retard
You smiled and said you knew but it was fun
We climbed a tree and there I took your hand
And with a razor blade I carved my name
In the pale flesh covered by your watchband
And then I rubbed your jeans until you came
Presently we reclined in the warm grass
And closed our eyes to look at our red lids
You said something I couldn't hear at last
We were confident and unworried kids
You jumped off the Eiffel Tower the year
I declared loneliness was my career.

Elizabeth Robinson — SONNET 25

i.e, I am not Ariel,
I am Caliban,
and sometimes it is very ugly.
—Paul Blackburn

What is this "world"? Its tender warmth
abets so few as they with their (gaudy) leaves unfurl, while this past decade
I've known such public humiliation that the world's gaze scorches me whose
native hardiness is now burnt, sharp. Sun-corroded blade, I
cut at what's been taken away, and still find the world's obdurate face
glaring at me. Was I so alone? Does that face beam solely on those whose
rewards are seasonal, but only seasonal? If so. World,

monstrous face, your very negligence gives means by which
your most obscure subjects rise, coequal as monsters. Where creature
meets creature and licit prizes fade from view. We—hidden, scratchy
beasts—consort here. Not beneath your sight but within it:
whose face our lips, our lobes, our furious hair. We are the very oil on your
skin as it gilds larger vision. All and better, we unknown who love and are
beloved where we may not be disclosed nor be removed.

Laynie Browne SONNET 26

26.1: An Abecedarian Translation Using only Text From the Original

All apparel as aspect bestows bare conceit
    But duty dares embassage
        Fair —good— graciously
    Guides hath head hope

How I knit   lord
Love mayst make me—
    Merit moving
Naked —not of points

Prove poor respect
    See some star strongly tattered
That thine thought till vassalage
    Wanting words where

Wit will witness
        Worthy   will

26.2 Translation of Abecedarian

Everything you put on reveals what you seek to hide

Something behind my face makes it dead—but only circumstantially

Are you obliged and do you dare to do what I'm not capable of?

Those trying to determine who they are—though we don't admit it—or have forgotten are also us

I want the written to ravish, even as it destroys me, against my own incendiary—

Don't worry about that riveting loss which carries you

You have no—choice—let it carve—close rivulets—in—

I'm writing this and you aren't even alive

As if it were embarrassing to be dead

You always exist in a rich enviable space

When the scorpion walked across my—hand

And I did not stop—the absence that goes on

Dawn—claws rough—clicking—benign—but coveting—elsewhere

Completely still and—seeing nothing—but visitation

Traver Pam Dick

SONNET 27

Brother-on-Sister, or I Do Georg: a Transonnet

0:01 Weary of self-willed, her-my fast bed, breeder, winter, self-killed, Obliterine. Breakdown, the shred you wear, shroud, worn-out book, argue-struggle-stir-disturb-a-crush-grind-dainty-poem-machine-for-crushing-peace-diminutive-for-hammered. Fair? Haste is violence-hatred-quarrel. Bed is to dig, I pierce, a grave. *Presumably a bed was dug out in the ground.* How-everything-could-be-one-word-but-with-hyphens. Like girl-boy-brother-lover. I said, 27 is my word-age. But I lied.

0:02 Deer-brother, posed phantom limb, brightness pricked in shifts, Trakl-travel. *Start* by breaking the rules. Like don't touch. Threshold. Later it will. Sometimes wrong. You can't put-it-back. Foliage-slanting-rod-torment-torture-instrument-with-three-suffering.

0:03 Bootless journeyman-outcast. Transient-world. Metallic-petal-mortal. But your strap-on prince! Begin, perhaps original, to open. A kin to yawn. Like you. Then just a head-trip? Yet transgress scorn, exalt.

0:04 But in my perturbed-clouds-rotten-smoke-transgrief-scars. Time killing. Why? You made me take my shirt off, and you promised. But splendor ≠ bravery. Drives-shame-motion. Then what breathes out, dies?

0:05 Thought's far-want, to fire you, email speed-*Lied*, slide-in-quicken. Though death-melancholy here. Fleeting-decomposition. Until recomposition. Await patience. Later, a patient. Poet makes what abides? Remain-continue-in-some-relationship-last-be-faithful. Until can't stand.

0:06 Ardor's intent slave-intension aims at you. Pilgrim-quest a stretch? Jealousy. That's your affair. But the clock. Say brother. We were two hands. Our small boat. Night-beautiful. Bitter-absence.

0:07 Only halfway, but already too much. Could it say, *Just shut up and fuck me?* Droop-weak, starved look, unslept, kept my I open. Nothing about the meanings.

0:08 Gaze dark, cop-feel you. Rival-writing. *Klar!* You are you. Blinding. *Does-he-need-you-like-I-do?* My friend. My small-rash-boat-on-your-waves. See, I, too, flirt. But oh. Darkness is to darken, hide. Ruin-decay.

0:09 My imaginary view fingers your base *Juwel*, everyone adores-adorns you. Music's mistranslation-deception. Toying. Toy. Your youth. Charm-fault. My bracelet-manacle. You-mine? No-hyphen-in-German-but-that's-a-fantasy. Meanwhile I only repeat the earlier-coupling.

0:10 Absent-straying-shadow, I'd yet wake tired you, *Dornröschen*, pricking. Give-present-present-gift. Unfaced-unseeing. Did time pass? Stain thicket. You can't sleep-me-off. Universe of disgrace. In you I'd put my all.

0:11 Or ghost, *jeweils* are you my night-vision, mountain-street-cloud-breezes-raven-owl-blackbird. Went for her jewel too quickly. She: little, merely fooling. Hung-up-on-her vs. her-hang-up. Fear. What's her spirit? My unreal-I-reeling-mind.

0:12 Black night, beauty's youth-untruth, unfair, still your ravening sister eyes. I'm alt. Undernourished. I am my night. Black akin to ink. Night means night. Face new-darkened. Obscurity-ignorance-sinfulness-misfortune-etc.

0:13 Low. My bare-will-private-cockiness would like others mine you. Same limb-of-argument. Night-and-day. My-limbs-*are*-my-mind. You love my name, mouth it, make me firm. Hold-my-nothing-something. Release me, let me go.

0:14 So for us unrest-madness, ill-hell-black-night-dark-rise-and-fall, until rhyme's quietus. I mean *our* rhyme's: I will you mine. Desire's death: quit it, brother! Our secret math. Equals knowing. Nil.

Insomniac Transonnet, Georg, I (Iambic Pent Remix)

1 Wore shred self-willed fast winter bed my/her
2 Deer-brother Trakl posed bright phantom limb,
3 Curse outcast head-trip says prince strap-on gear,
4 Perturbed cloud mortal petal transgrief grim.
5 Want's email speed-*Lied* patient. Staying? Think.
6 Slave heat wait stretch-quest night's hands jealous clock
7 Could say shut up and kiss me? Slept not. Blink;
8 Gaze dark cop-feel but rival blind cock-block,
9 Imagined jewel your charm-fault. Base toy,
10 *Dornröschen* pricking. Thick time. Stray or sink,
11 My night views *jeweils* you hung up destroy
12 Untruth's black youth eyes raven sister ink,
13 Mouth my name, my shaft would like them mine you,
14 So mad unrest til quietus rhymes: through.

A brief conclusion to this sonnet providing insight into its actual form/possible meaning, word constraint replacing syllable constraint, 27 Trakl's age at suicide, 14 lines dividing evenly by 11 into 154 sonnets, lay this sonnet across the entire sonnet sequence because craving the whole because insatiable because addicted, choose one out of every set of 11 sonnets to cross with each line of this sonnet, the two sonnets fucking, exchanging spit, sounds, words, and swallowing the explanatory notes aka glossary or taking it into yourself so now they are not explanation but expatiation and inside the sonnet itself instead of outside facing it as in my copy of his book, so in violation of distinction or boundary as in incestuous poetics including mistranslation, likewise how the fair youth actually is the dark lady, dual aspect but transformation of view, or how the male is female or the sister could be the brother or two versions of the same sonnet, sonnet meaning poem/sound, and the second or sister version metrical/syllabic/rhyming i.e. overtly musical like Grete, and trying for the convention but it will be briefer than Georg's life, and how sonnet 27 actually continues into 28 since they are two linked sonnets, although she was 26 when she committed suicide 3 sections i.e. years later, so 26 could in fact follow 27 as in 26 parts of the one sentence or *Satz* or musical movement of this brief conclusion like the brief introduction in my copy of the sonnets, here the last will not be first but will act like it, mean like it, in the ending is the act, there being more that could be said but then the limit's reached, so there's self-silencing.

Judith Goldman

SONNET 28

[DRAFT: not for circulation]

#########CANCELLED: SONNET 28###########

To: Fiery Orb: "THE.ONLIE.BEGETTER"
From: Will
Cc: Nighttime
Re: Palinode [Day-for-night (beta)]

Sun woke me this morning loud and clear, "
Time was
You deleted 28. Dummy files, too!
Write that atlas of Atlantis, Lunar Baedeker to last—
But this! Pilot-less, God your co-drone. Without needing to look.
Plus what about Phil: Here you coineth not, but spend a coin.
You're not making your own days.
This token wld not survive the bite: it wanted to be haunted,
But you must admit its ghost barely gave itself spirit,
Power base in waste.
So what can it hurt to decommission effigy of effigy, that bore
Commodity's hurried blur even before
We followed it to Hell? It's one thing to tear
an eagle from the sky, another to throw a little doll down a well.
Capisce?"

Waking up in the hotseat's bound
to make one prone

to excuses. To make an oak sweat, when his card's declined.
Take it out the rotation? If I was like, No, ye flames, I'll tell ye how to burn, or,
Doe thou stande, Sunne, in some by-roome, while I question my puny drawer,
etc. Makes him look bad, makes the grass stick in his throat, now
my
heliocentric
recantation
demanded is.
I'd claim innocence but How
can I be innocent/
If I do not know the charge? E'en if
with my own ramrod stuff'd?
If it looks like a rifle but the barrel isn't rifled, it's not a rifle,
It's a musket. And when is a musket not a muskrat.
Sun says it's none my flock.
So I remit:
Pardon the low res, I ripped it.
And having sworn myself in,
I fire in salute and tell
the shabby gag in full.
Taking Sun for Day, and Night for Night,
We must as well take
Will's 28 for Phil's 89, and there's the rub:
Sidney's songlet 'gat my zombie autonomic,
A Headless, heedless allegory
Since the Sidney's without head, blueprint unhinged. Sun's
Angry at the copula:
A Subject cannot predicate
with counterfeit of counterfeit
A gift burlesques commodity
As moon of sun is parody;
Just as in shadow this be writ

And so by imitation lit –
Do ye marvell at my droll tetrapaks? as I wax
Procrustean,
taking a foot at my Inn. In short, I'm not to hold any rung
of this degraded ladder. You'd think that Day comes once a day
But Phil's pegged Apollo Bacchus, Day comes and comes again. They say love's born of poverty, yet all the same, the rime's too *riche*, and this is just what's made it poor. When bill's receipt, accompts cannot be scored, Time bores its tunnel into the future. Clothed in japery's drapery I may have been, but you'll soon see the joke's for true: "Now that of absence the most irksome night, / With darkest shade doth overcome my day; / Since Stella's eyes, wont to give me my day, / Leaving my hemisphere, leave me in night, / Each day seems long, and longs for long-stay'd night; / The night as tedious, woos th'approach of day; Tir'd with the dusty toils of busy day." You see? Let me fill an ocean with a dropper 'ere I (this sentence signed: Too Bored To Finish). Oddly enough, it knows itself some Strange form of battalogia, talking of the toilsome and tedious. *Bunny rabbit* is a word composed of 2 words, where both of the words mean the same thing, and the word composed of both of the words also means the same thing. The very everything. When hacked I Sidney to his capital, I took the dingus, das ding. Yet had to blunt, disedge, its turnless plot. Its undynamic dynamite. And e'en so, retract I must? Ok, Sun, here's my rewrite, I've put a grain to wood:

This sonnet hangs its three-ball sign out front:
To Pawnbroke, Broken 'pon this shopworn trope.
Rise early, get your Phil: day's Conny c***,
For Stella's buck stopped here, beyond her hope.
I'll not hang a debt on debt 'til books spew gold.
Collapsed archive's a wrecker's yard for parts—
This junked junket all all-alike, all told.
Unzipped the language from its crease in starts
And fits, less fit I found it on review!

Such fun to ring around a leaden Saturn!
My ontological predation sue
If I don't limper wring this songlet slattern.
Here's my *Lettre de Course*: I'm corsair true,
I scratch escutcheon, arbitrage: SuperValue.

'Tis confession, but no apology. Improvement? It's no *Macbeth*: "Come, thick night, And pall thee in the dunnest smoke of hell, That my keen knife see not the wound it makes, / nor heaven peer through the blanket of the dark, / To cry 'Hold, hold!'"; "has sat i' the stocks all night…"; "And on your finger in the night I'll put…"; "Come, night; end, day! For with the dark, poor…" Great and inky lines of night (hendiadys my signature, go figure). . . . .
. . . .
. . . .
. . . . In 28, double of 27, double of Phil's 89 (*supra ref*), there's lines that all read wrong, re: their (Day and Night's) colluded Torture of one Me: "And each, though enemies to either's reign / Do in consent shake hands to torture me; / The one by toil, the other to complain / How far I toil, still farther off from thee." Every critic writes that "swart-complexion'd night" forces me to consider how far I am from my Boy Love. If we unMoor the Dark, to drop anchor where it will, we still
have Day as Seer, taskmaster, Night as Lambaster
of mine Sisyphean works. A Hypocrite Night, since Night
undo unduly all.
Let us Now rethink defiles o' the pitchy night.
The Now that is Night is preserved, i.e. it is treated as what it professes to be, as something that is; but it proves itself to be, on the contrary, something that is not. The Now does indeed preserve itself, but as something that is not Night; equally it preserves itself in face of the Day that it now is, as something that also is not Day, in other words as a negative in general. To cast forth a seed of corn is "sowing" but to cast forth its flame, as is said of the sun, has no special name. . .
. . . . Sun

vomits its light, the little quids, too many flags. Night as Day's mental darkness, *als ob* Sun shon
thru Cloth of dark's sad shreds for stars, Attic chorus
thrown back on. Spirit pushing through the flesh, yeoman, citoyen. It's all you. Arraying oneself in the open
space. Photo-Electric univocity, thermal monad, circulus incessant. Nice kicks. The fucking motherboard.
Took some snaps: Sun in grot. Sun out in yard. Sun set.
And Night, you wineless cup. Angel of an-other religion, wings clipped in negation. Your jagged solidarity buildout or slum. Towards which
this world was bleeding. Corpsed Being and its ways of Being. Has to be that way? Shittern Night, Night errant, you've never Been
Inside your own skin. Propped on the actual thing of it, void by cut created. Bupkis.
How shift night, Now the Night Shift? Crossstreet Dusk, or Dawn.
"Black site" to comptroll Sun as universal solvent. Sun winded on spindle of Night: Porter it no longer, Sky, as hung on thread of light. I have jess of Sun (Status Update: "noonless day"; "halp!"), Day's Inn. Asteroid.
My poem all caesura, canceled Heliography.
Posterity remark its debt.
The light spills over, solar cyst, spiral jutty, this cant luster, glister,
Night and Day, Live or Die, call thought back to its sting. They are already at the door.
Sun, are you a star, adjunct to Night, riven in it? Night, the Real Subsumption of it?
To offer its own syntax, creation by subtraction: we get to know the law of its refraction, not
a mere surface, contrary to my purpose. Stars, are you Night's immaculate ejaculate?
And so says Night, did I
Solicit thee
From darkness to promote me?
To inly entify? I ride the differences, un-face, reverb;

it will be by sheer luck that I happen on the truth! Rough argument ensues:

. . . .

One morning as the sky was already growing light…

betimes

(as so many ontological specks, rebegot of not)

And Now if you'll/as we complete the circuit,
candescing rusted wanderlust

A bit too fast you melt this wax.

Adieu.
WS

Like this:LikeBe the first to like this

cancellation onclick="javascript:_gaq.push(['_trackEvent','outbound-article'

Matthea Harvey

SONNET 29

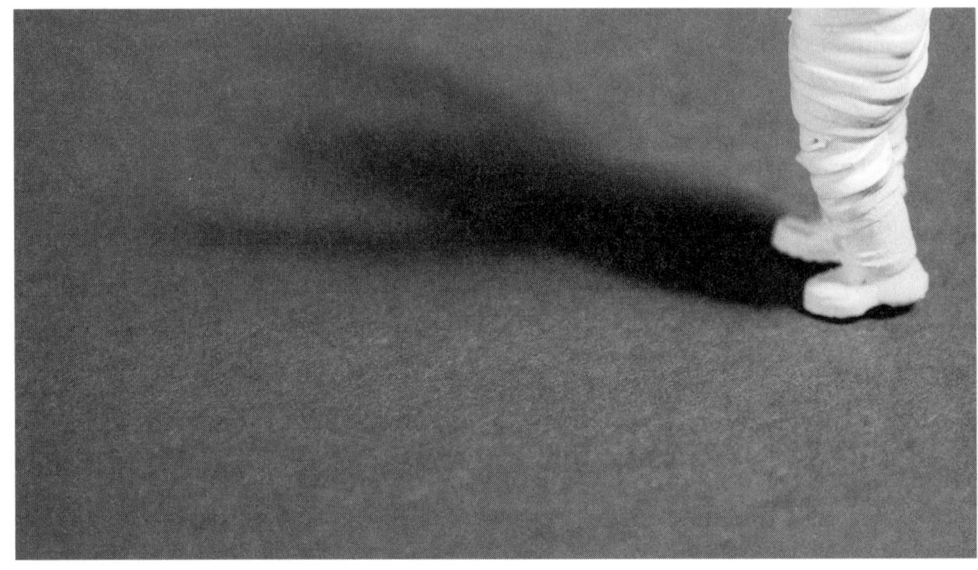

Michelin Man Possessed by William Shakespeare

I've taken many forms over the years,
but this may be the strangest one. I see
through his eyes but cannot shed a tear,
I can feel his feet, but am not free
to leave this spot by the garage. I think
he feels a kind of love for the balloon
who bobs nearby. Each day he sees her sink
an inch. Though I want to tell him of the moon
and slippered feet in marble halls, these tires
at our waist are a mischief. I make believe
they are couplets of rubber, but barbed wire
would be more apt. It's very hard to breathe.
Make us a man, or make us a machine—
but do not leave us trapped here in-between.

Eric Zboya

SONNET 30

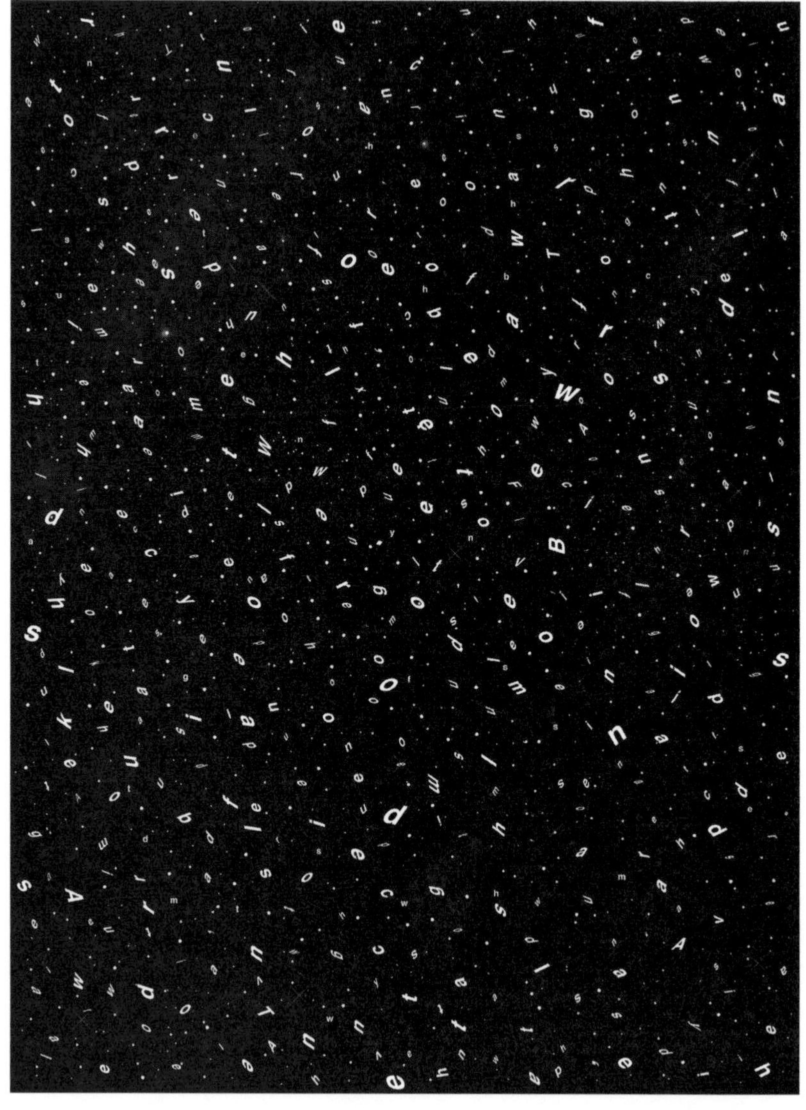

Laura Wetherington — SONNET 31

We are looking for.
Council life.
Love and warmth.
I will be happy.
An experience.
The book is a religion in the snow.
No.
No!
He was Buried with his sword.
I have a price list.

more

First, it is.

Will Edmiston

SONNET 32

Their love inhabit past me
whiff shalt line deaths
flood time in thy bones
shalt ye jahi nuff respect
yunk to né needle normal
sea-high waist. More private.
Dearer alter ni for strengths
deep turn in, turn em in knots
xample shores xalter thine
              Corsage
through wheres
friend-love kind of raise
  out the day
  fine fine in the fine ray

Sara Wintz

SONNET 33

there is a morning that
expresses the mountaintops
green in the eyes of the golden face
are the grasses

pale streams shaken world
eyeball planet, o
sun, look west with
triumphant splendor at my brow
for one hr you were mine

the sun
clouds regionally mask
yet i love him for this
people make stains
like heaven

Ann Cotten

SONNET 34

Why it's so nice
me cold ok ok
and then an ugly spice:
you face you turn away
and then turn back
and touch my lip
that is no cure
for what you bit
and now you pout
it is no better
you still were bad to me
i shiver still
you love me not
give me your sweater

Cedar Sigo

SONNET 35

XXXV

Fuck off with your crippling guilt
The earth has edges, boys get thrown in fountains
Dusk is painted over the moon, the sun grows black in your sleep
Peel back your lotus to its bloody root
No one is beyond reproach except the indians
And still I twist your fault against my grip
My head spins when the old bull rushes
Fills your whore bath past the brim of night
I suffer this reversal right beside you
I talk myself out of the song, I plead
Go to the sea, the lake, the tree,
hear the acid burn round my skull
You're so fine I still play dumb
A zombie dust inside your lungs
Draw me in deeper with deceit and smoke, lets go again

Brandon Shimoda

SONNET 36

I have to go I have to tell—
You—Turn from me—Summon new
Intoxications (1) Through
Me—Please—What
Does not please me—Once
Even—Or—Our (2)
Selves will sucker an intoxicating gel
As like but not—Exactly—Orange (3)
Feminines chiming in on "India" Day (4)
Have to for bringing back what originally was
That I—Will not look back
On—I (5) Or other—
Wise—Imitations never and not
Looking back (6) But down
You hate the idea don't you—Carrying differently
In—To solus poison (7) Under
Judging upon the standing block the dead
Sowing incantations (8) With—While—Power
May profess—Mega-poetry possessing—It
Is (9) Shameful to mention
What the disobedient do
When separated—Threaded through (10)
Pubic hair teased from adults disposed
By nature—On—Or in (11) Assimilating
Pubic hair—I wake to
Angelic art-making sacrifices (12)
Unlocking defense tools—Rocking roses
You are pleasing—What (13) Pleases
Will double and pour back—To—You—Will
Pour your body out—Though not
To you or me—To—Wives— (14)

Maxine Chernoff

SONNET 37

Hymn

father's delight
child's deeds
Fortune's spite
comforts truth
beauty's wit
these all
do crown
engrafted store
I am
shadow's substance
thy abundance
thy glory
look best
this wish

Ana Božičević

SONNET 38

14 Fragments/10 Muses

We're with James Baldwin in a lofty basement room, with a narrow strip of windows close to the ceiling revealing a moving stream of star-sky. There's a loud high-pitched sound in the room. "Oh that?" James says. "That's just the stars howling."

Me and Sampson Starkweather are making a poem. It goes:

"Beauty is just a series of essays
proving that beauty doesn't exist."

I'm staying in the same B&B as Matvei Yankelevich did some ten years ago with a young, moon-faced woman, who is referred to as his "bride." On the washroom mirror, I find pinned a poem, titled "The Stag and Doe," that begins:

"In the winter, when the moon is pinched…"

I understand the destruction of this poem will end Matvei's sadness.

I have successive night-long conversations with Dodie Bellamy and TC Tolbert.

Diane di Prima says: "We danced the dream, and then our dream exploded: '71, '72, '73, '74."

I'm in a village in winter, sheltered in the cottony silence of a cottage. There is no electricity; not just here, but anywhere in the world. Amy King is with me. I tell her:

"And since it's the time
before fabric, since neither of us bows, I guess
I'll braid your hair forever."

Amy and I are on our way to a demonstration for the murder of a young man. We meet up with Metta Sama. We are all wearing hoodies of "goddess wool." Metta explains, "They've murdered our desire."

Bhanu Kapil puts out a call on her blog for people to send her contributions: either in the "ephemeral language" or in the "language of the dead," which she calls Forban.

I receive a Ziploc bag of pressed dead butterflies. It's from Vanessa Place. On the very white wings of the largest one is written: "Wittgenstein for Ana." When I wake, I think, "OK," go to the shelf and open the *Tractatus* at random. It says:

"It is only in so far as a proposition is logically segmented that it is a picture of a situation."

Filip Marinovich

SONNET 39

Divided Live

Sister
Sister was looking at me and I said why are you
looking at me?
She says Well why do you think I'm looking at you.
She's sitting in a chair I'm standing.
I kneel down as she says this and/or after
she says it. We hug each other and deep.
My face is mashed in her long black rough hair.
I'm wet. We are both high and drunk from
Belgrade marijuana and Belgrade home made liquor
and Belgrade air with that special uranium rain tang scent.
Bent. We kiss each other. We begin to kiss.
When we were kids the adults told us
to kiss each other that we were brother and sister.
Now we are at each other. We are listening. We
are finally listening now and that is good.
We are being obedient obedienter
than they ever might've wanted us to be.
We are pressing against each other wet and we
get to the bed undress each other and feel each other and I ask her
Do you have a condom she says No we don't need a condom
we're just going to use our hands so we do we use our hands
on each other until we come first her then me when she comes

Brian Teare

SONNET 40

OCCUPY SONNET

Why turn a lover's discourse into a discourse about debt? The sonnet begins with a complaint: if I've already given you all my money, then—duh—you've got it all. But sonnets and lovers depend on numbers. We tried to explain this to the credit card companies, but it didn't work. Both poet and lover enumerate, count with their fingers: syllables, kisses, both stressed and unstressed. We tried to explain this to the banks, but it didn't work. The success of writing a sonnet or of loving rests on neither being too idle about counting, nor too attached to the act of counting itself. We tried to explain this to the federal government, but our calls couldn't get through. Such idleness might indicate a lack of ardor or insufficient intellectual engagement; over-investment in the numbers might indicate a lack of trust or insufficient imagination. We tried to explain this to the president, but the woman on the 27 bus told us: "He thinks dick is stronger than money, but *we* know money is stronger than dick." A good writer or lover knows the true value of what they're counting, but it's debt when the beloved says, "What you have given me is not enough." A few of us began to protest. "Poverty is something money can't buy," Joanne says, but it can be stolen when it's a metaphor. The sonnet's complaint continues: I've given you all I had, and now you've taken more, what the fuck? Some of us kept working three jobs and making payments on time. This is an example of what the literary critic calls "the masochism of the abjectness of love." Some of us who later joined the occupation were taking out student loans or were still unemployed or had lost homes to foreclosure. Such theft can only be forgiven when debt is a lover's playful fiction, an accounting that amounts to nothing spent but wit. Some of us were vets unable to get proper psychiatric care; some of us had lost access to medical treatments our health depended on. When poverty is literal and persistent, it's an injury we learn to live with without forgiveness. Some of us wanted to, but couldn't join the protests, and sent cookies or money or words of support, whatever we could spare in the hours we weren't working or looking for work. The sonnet goes on to argue something like: the problem with numbers is that when we have plentitude, we tend to forget the experience of lack or find it threatening. National networks send us images of violent confrontations; from Oakland Miranda and Eirik send us images of peaceful actions; Brenda reminds us "we are agents for something greater than ourselves." The problem with the ones obsessed with numbers above all else is that counting offers endless labor that replaces all other activities. Counting confers an illusion of value when in reality it is by itself all but worthless; it confers an illusion of total order when in reality the one who counts has had to forget their knowledge of everything between us that can't be converted to currency. On the train beneath Wall Street, a sleek pinstriped financier falls asleep with his cheek against my shoulder. Under rush hour fluorescence I see his pallor, a patch of stubble beneath his jaw where his morning razor didn't make it; I see his grip on his leather briefcase slowly slacken. The concluding couplet makes a concessionary gesture: because of the contradiction alive in everything, I see it will be necessary to love the ones who don't yet know how gravely they have wounded us, if only because soon their dream will stop, the doors will open and they will wake up in our arms.

Christina Davis

SONNET 41

Love is so early in us: it is the earliest and
therefore no wonder it is a child. And
Shakespeare a child, an earliness of Us,
and also a father of license and also a chider
of the flesh where fib and freedom meet,
and his syntax so soon that his "art" is now
"are" again, and "thy" outgrown the rhyme
with "ay," and "I" is not Will but a bothness,
a two-foldness of master-mistress-lover-friend.
He is/we are long since translated into a larger
belonging, a past-tenseness of Genesis, and all
infidelities have returned from that first tree
which exists only in so far as I am still a verb
and you are still and go and come to me.

Douglas Kearney

SONNET 42

you getting her doesn't get me though you heard I hurt for her.
yet her getting you hurts me because you got me right *there*
and I got you right *here*. I get it though, you're hurting for her
because I hurt for her and I get her hurting for you for me
though it hurts, hearing your hurting for her hurts her
for me. I hurt because you're not here but you get to be
hers, and my not getting her gets her there as yours. her
and you, I get, get you and her, your *our*. I get *their* but no *our*
there. I get your *there there* for me, and I get got for you and her
your. but get this: you got me *there* and I got you *here*,
so your *your* is my *mine*. hear, hear her hurting for yours is mine
there where yours is *here* so there's no *your there* only mine, right?

Daniel Tiffany

SONNET 43

When most I wink, then do mine eyes best see,

For all the day they view things unrespected;

But when I sleep, in dreams they look on thee,

And darkly bright are bright in dark directed.

Then thou, whose shadow shadows doth make bright,

How would thy shadow's form form happy show

To the clear day with thy much clearer light,

When to unseeing eyes thy shade shines so!

How would, I say, mine eyes be blessed made

By looking on thee in the living day,

When in dead night thy fair imperfect shade

Through heavy sleep on sightless eyes doth stay!

All days are nights to see till I see thee,

And nights bright days when dreams do show thee me.

Nate Pritts

SONNET 44

Outside it's not as damaged
as anyone expected & people
seem disappointed that life
is safe again. They wanted it to be epic
since just going to the grocery
makes us feel normal.
At least with all this rain
one appreciates a new color scheme.
The trees are calm & dull
in their substance. Each plop of rain
is injurious to each nimble leaf.
Green is still green even when
the atoms don't refract the same
or there is such different light. Jenny
what do you think about this
tradition of the poet writing to the muse,
the actual beloved missing?
What about people always wishing
for the worst so that they have
something to talk about? I can be
sitting in our current pretty relaxed
circumstances &, pow!, my mind settles
on the farthest earth remov'd from me.
My thoughts are lingering
some other where. Like Brooklyn
or Asheville or Lafayette
while obviously drenched in Syracuse
& it kills me to be so out of whack.
Like people who are glad to read about

disasters as if their life or their fear
finally has reason. Jenny, maybe
there is such a thing as intrinsic qualities.
Am I a good person meant for a good life?
Describe the place where you are
& what makes it a refuge in your thoughts.
Is that feeling transferable?
I am having a hard time getting the tone
right in this poem. Maybe it's okay
to have different feelings all at once.
You wake up blinking the ghost of strong light
from your eyes & feeling exuberant
despite the dense & slow moisture in the air.

Michelle Taransky

SONNET 45

The other sue, slight air encouraging higher
A both within be wherever and at first sight are
We honor lives insider
These precedents accidents limit swift motions filed
For way use waiting for ailments are calm
Instead they're analysts see below city
My in my being made about four with stubborn homes
Sing stance again oppressed with missing moneys
And so less composition being Richard
But by a stripped messengers return to a me
To evening but now come back again and share it
Our and fire's power recounting exceedingly
This trial, we'd surely but bend no longer collapse
Coming mended and then and straightened both sent

This translation was transcribed from the closed-captioning Youtube assigned to my first attempt reading Shakespeare's Sonnet 45 "together" with Victoria Gamerman.

Tyrone Williams

SONNET 46

Condemned: a public property by dint
of blood before am out. Yet out—
          yanked back—
kow-towed to mine hysteric, cold-
cocked by mine asunder. Not yet out
mine eyes negate negation: am pursued
as am pursued: mine meet- thine mate- née help
around a blind curve: ampersand
of moiety-cum-moiety.
                              But cut
cut corners—back—not out—for blood, mine back
into it notwithstanding. Didn't make
a dent in it, the public held.
                                        Brought up
on charges—was to be—indicted. Peers
impaneled née mine peeps. Bipartisan
republic, charge to verdict: kiss the Built.

Marcella Durand & Betsy Fagin SONNET 47

The translation took place 9/9/11 between 5:45 and 6:30 pm in the Whispering Gallery in Grand Central Terminal. Marcella Durand and Betsy Fagin each took turns reading the sonnet into a corner, with their voice carrying diagonally over the curve of the gallery's ceiling to the opposite corner, to be then transcribed. Train announcements, rush hour ambient noise and tourists using the gallery simultaneously disrupted and enriched the translation that had particular words ringing as percussion.

Between mine eye and   heavily is
divine courage now come to mine
when not mine eye vanish work
hard in love tied   what?
With my sticks   and my eyes
down state   & to the recent anchor
fits my heart   another time is
my eye   my heart   and in the body
sharing   so either I love or
thyself   thy art stormy for
thou not farther   thoughts
& they are still
for all I have seen
my picture   whisper whisper
eyes   heart

—BF to MD (SW corner)

Betwixt mine eye
a league is took   turns out
+ that mine eye was banished
for look   + sighs
with love's picture
what injured other times
arts suggest
guards of love
either by thy pleasure
or love
myself
for thou not eyes
canst
hearts + eyes delight

—MD to BF (SW corner)

Betwixt my eye & heart anemic
& even doth return now unto the
                                                                other
when mine eye   vanishes
                                                                                forward
in part of love's sigh
soft
with my love pick mine
                        eye of peace
it fits my heart
another time my eye is
                        bearing just
mine heart
for eye to eye   picturing my mug
for now a light allows
an eye that sees
if they see my picture
of my heart   my heart

—BF to MD (NE corner)

Betwixt mine eye + heart
each turns now to the other
+ that mine eye is famished
love w/ sighs that
doth my loves picture eye
painted back heart
+ other tunes my eyes
heart loves share heart
so either by thy pictures
still w/ me
now thoughts
eye still
with them sleep
wakes my heart
to heart's + eyes' delight

—MD to BF (NE corner)

Lee Ann Brown

SONNET 48

The Lower 48 (Je Ne Regrette Rien)

How anally I took my way with you
Each little tweak on the badass thrust
so that I would not be tempted to use you up
False hands made you a ward of the state of things

To you, my churl, my jewels were just dessert,

Most close-held hope, you broke my neck.

You were my love forever, so close, you *were* me,

but left high and dry, art stole you from me

I never locked you in no iron maiden

You put yourself there, out of reach for art

I pull poems from inside of me

Did you ever take the pleasure that was yours?

Evaporation: a prize, so feared

I am afraid to open my eyes

Stacy Szymaszek

SONNET 49

against history
(untold)
I surmise

and offer
small
repair

the low slung
head of
needs

I am your new mother

with defects you'll
never perceive

a gift of
breeding

how could I
come audit time

convert my
loyalties to
love

you are Rome and Paris and Newcastle on Tyne
you are life savings

unworthy of care
unworthy to care
the city in twos
thank god

an ethic
that mobilizes
love in the absence
of eye contact

our red crosses lock
and gleam

the hound at twilight
refuses another
new name

Mathias Svalina

SONNET 49

Wastoid

A man put his man on one arm of an enormous balancing scale. On the other arm the first man put a pair of colorful cowboy boots. The second man was heavier than the colorful boots. The first added a fluffy purple party dress but the second man was still heavier than the boots & dress. Then the first removed one of his legs & added it to the second arm. Still, the second man was heavier. Then the first removed his other leg & added it but the second man was still heavier. Then the first removed his arms & added them to the scale but the second man was heavier still. Then a large police officer wandered in & stepped up on the second arm of the scale in order to steal the colorful cowboy boots. This tipped the scale & the first man nodded, slowly, serenely, as if this was what he had always expected. The police officer wandered away. The first man began to cry. The second man stepped off of the scale, picked up the first man's arms & attached them to his own body, just below his first set of arms, as the first man continued to lie on the concrete. Then the first man's first set of hands held tightly to his other set of hands.

Sharon Mesmer

SONNET 50

With what heavy-hued wino joy do I journey—ahoy, diva!
Like a weatherman who knows his whiskey, and the mystery of "Hee Haw,"
I have tats with teeth that suck Death's mopey toe . . .
Thus are my miles measured, friend: by all the fun, fail and weird things going
Around on Facebook, and beyond.
And they plod dully on, to bear the weight of wonking twins,
As if by Stinktown's cybernetic knits this wretch could know
Her rider, who so famously loved the overbold syrupy taste
Of way hormonal light-duty trucks.
But I doth mistrust morons, nostrums, the stated mission of Master Trout—
To cripple voter registration activity—which he insists is monism,
An inmost rumor of sharp tits that spur the sides;
For that same hypnotism romps thuddingly in my mind,
As my grief lies onward, and my joy behind.

Martha Ronk

SONNET 51

1.

From thee, to thee, from where, here is, not now, then when,
no more, no horse, no flesh, nay neigh, go forth, come back
trotting along, writing a wit, slowing perforce, lacking excuse,
coming along, bearing a beast, pacing the act, mounting the wind,
willfully fast, hasting it hence, spurring it on [then] not finished yet
winding it down, finally, my love, only dull flesh, "of posting no need."

2.

Thus can
Of my
From where
Till I
O, what
When   Then
In Then
Therefore
Thus shall
. . . . .   I go.

3.

The repetition of events isn't a matter of will, more often
a matter of passive resistance to the overwhelming pleasure
of concocting excuses or revising the phrases
after pacing the carpets from one hallway to the other,
dragging one's heels on the worn explanations,
one choice barely outweighing another in the scheme of things—
time itself the bloody culprit
such as that all that makes sense isn't speed or retard
but gauging the limbo, repeating, reversing, in hopes
of perfecting one's manner, one's means of seduction.

Heather Christle

SONNET 52

As Translated by Maxwell's Demon

aaaaa aaaaa aaaaa aaaaa aaaaa aaaBB Bbbbb
bbbCc ccccc ccccc ccccd ddddd ddddd dddde
eeeee eeeee eeeee eeeee eeeee eeeee eeeee
eeeee eeeee eeeee eeeee eeeee eeeee eeeFf
fffff ggggg ggghh hhhhh hhhhh hhhhh hhhhh
hhhhh hhhhh Iiiii iiiii iiiii iiiii iiiii
iiiii iiiij kkkkk kLlll lllll lllll lllll
lmmmm mmmmm mmmnn nnnnn nnnnn nnnnn nnnnn
oooo oo oo oo oo oo oo oo oo oo oo oo oo oo oO On nn nn
rrrrr rrrrr rrrrr rrppp ppppp ppppp ooooo
sssss sssss sssss sssss sSSSr rrrrr rrrrr
ttttt ttttt ttttT TTsss sssss sssss sssss
wwvvv uuuuu uuuuu ttttt ttttt ttttt ttttt
....- -,,,, ,,,,, ,yyyy yyyyy ywwww wwwww

Rusty Morrison

SONNET 52

sonic fig juice

somatic bitch-boy in the under-words, hissing bestialities—
can't beat it, cheesy sock-puppet leisure—
witch me, heathen, knock me loud into surgery—
forethoughts buried, dime-joint mind in cellular seizure—
wherefore, sore of fealty to feasibility, stupor-swollen, sucking air—
wince! the poem's not even nearly half done yet—
yikes! my groaning words, thought-hearses, waste escape valves—
oh capacious germs, can't sterilize my shtick or sex it—
sewed into quick lime, that old rhymer that shaking-spear gent—
I've an oar behind my earlobe, for beating back the talktide—
tumored with orneriness, I am spurious, I am hesitation-blasted—
buy it new here, infatuation is the poem's best incendiary lie—
howl-beatified in the 50s, come to surrounded by ad-marketing & lyric-dopers—
getting had, tho, is my fav trumpet, singing lag-time, blindly I grope—

Zach Savich

SONNET 53

the worn grass between restaurant and motel

is refreshed to green again

as restraint can open into

oh well   by your natural darkness

it renders any glass

into a mirror we pass

and who can blame some other

touching herself

in the shape of the shade you are

reflective in

—

the mechanic's a florist now

too   arranging

orchids in

tires bedazzled to look after you

—I want to call it spring already

you say, *every shadow's the shadow*

of the same thing

—

let's make an eggplant

let's go jump in a lake

let's lose our shirt

don't you think everything

would be a good name

for a flower

as branches braid and bear fruit

underground   faithful

to fertility that does not   only reproduce but continually

makes itself

so everywhere I went

in spring the spring

had already been

ditches concealed in unseasonal abundance

how about some tea

how about loving me forever

—

also

the taste on your tongue

is not too sweet

it's simply sugar

—

also

the day looks lovely on you

it's so like you

near horses breaking

into their corralled trot   in abruptly breaking

rain   beautiful   if you like that kind of thin

Brenda Iijima

SONNET 54

Oh, methane *secretly gassing off* the basins minding
And quiet mounds of quietly discarded ornaments
Glittering in the dirt, a pain secreting. The rose upon the broken
Clock looking epic and corrupt as it meets a doll
Head and an empty water bottle sticking out amongst the rot.
Hard deaths the cruelest landfill does the little town create.
Godbwye my little portion of junk and refinery.
Our deaths will precede you glowingly and severely by at
Least 200 calibrated years as presences fade into animal
By coastlines and hills elaborated with words and little
Cries. Dirt is such a responsive material that's quietly alive
And eating. Oh, wondrous dirt, perform a quiet quieted
Wasting of these post-consumer remains. The perfumed
Reality of fuming space is distilling, quietly distilling, oh you

Geoffrey G. O'Brien

SONNET 55

No type of matter can preserve itself
Or keep a noun away from its verb form,
So Shakespeare will prefer the abstract shelf
Where bodies made of words are safe from harm.
The poem's two key words are *not* and *this*:
Beginning with negating material things
And ending with the poem's nothingness
That *this* refers to as the poem sings
Its end, and makes of song a dwelling place
Where one can play the object of address
To enter speech where bodies fail in space.
The contents are the only weakness
The sonnet will admit it needs to live,
A contradiction ending won't forgive

But sonnets don't quite end, they conclude.
And is the sonnet over? Yes, and yes and no:
We've outlived rhyme and gilded endings
And content's monuments, but not this form
Persisting as a limit, fourteen lines
The record still finds room for; the form
Survives its features by outpacing them
Inside itself, needing only eyes
To overturn all death until mere subject,
Like love. As subjects both are pretexts for
An exploration of the form, as facts
The motivation for experiment
With *not* and *this*, outliving using them
So type can matter without mattering.

Mary Jo Bang

SONNET 56

LVI

They said: ocean parts the shore; do not love
love. So sweet, summer's wished see
where two come to be. Tomorrow, dullness—
the interim-like contracted view, the new
perpetual winter. Call it, your hungry appetite
banks in care today that which is tomorrow
fullness blest with sharpened blunter. Although
your love might renew the welcome allayed
this, or a full of spirit which, which may be
rare, the be-edge should not be: thrice daily let
your kill-eyes fill till they wink. When today
makes you return, more by force of being you
than of his former love—you see and be more
again, but with even more sad feeding it.

Joshua Marie Wilkinson

SONNET 57

And Under

Being at the knees of what's come out from
under the weight of the cloaked, clocked how
I listed vacant till winter's slot thrash recessed, though
nor can I visitant-up through a page
nor arrest any long-clicked back attentions
whilst distracting myself with pictures, from pictures—
nor with you, simply unworried about the moment
when our histories surpass toxin and blear, yet fuse yearning.
Nor would any single taste from here carry us off to
where we thought desire meant us to go
but listening with one's mechanisms torched
save the loves who battered us beyond free
so I wanted what I came to forget
and you showed me just what I dragged from it forth.

Gillian Conoley

Son 8

god made me your slave
thought control times
account crave,
vassal stay,
O let me suffer
(being at your beck)
absence of your library,
tame check,
injury be,
you list, your self, your time
to what you belong,
self-doing I am
wait, hell blame
your pleasure ill, well

Corina Copp

SONNET 59

<<My face in thine eye, and thine
in mine>> is true speech, and is
I read naturally, is male, and
if, I did not look but basketfuls
of presumptive eggs all wet
do nothing for us playing at it.
If and is don't lack for harmless
napkins like freed, unending
time bleats through the
washed away. In mine, suns
dulcet polishing of a tlooth,
<<as much falsity as I can use,
I carry.>> On the level, a prop-
osition to disrobe contra shit
on the streets steams near a hot-
spot a relationship a sign a man
pinned to your back moves a
name I'd armament but you know
in a flageolet sitch I'd do any-
thing for you so. On the level?
She ran her car aground as his
ships firing agony in sand mag-
netized black screens of mites,
her car OK tho, it hurts, hood-
winked and The Image in Form is
a book of art writing by Adrian
Stokes and also in Malina,
the fact is <<I've never been
happy, but I have seen beauty.>>

What a fine replacement.
Blubbery and dying in my
same as breastbone for you
is some fixed charge waiting for
Papermate to stir a con-
ditional tense apparition, or
is that a coffee, tedious wall
clouds are rather of soap, see
and hath sense since torment
and hydromancy bothered to tune.
More, more if must be, more if I'd
be into it, I said I'd do whatever.
What would she of the unmistake-
ably Gothic appearance write
me, <<I'm losing my mind with
probity presumably forever,>> sure,
I like most care more than fuck-
ing Tiffany's rattle, inlaid with
let's book it to Alpine, if a diviner
knew you then too as I do.
I wish she would tell me what
to do with you, or if I did look,
How marvelous to see you,
post-screening, makes <<true
hearts in plain faces rest>>
more larding and accurate?
Or whether revolution be the same.
In 1938, hotspot was employed
in the firefighting sense and
whitish smoke employment gives
other women illustrates finitude
onscreen, a labor of demand.

If other women wanted finitude
over touchable repetition or if I
beat and beat salad or roast new
potatoes deeply in salt and oil
and exclaim their spits as an otter
might shriek the slightest un-
attitude vocable across your
hunks in Pisces comportment, or
with happens in trying and apts.
to go mad in, surely it's been
nothing near this terrific face
I never in real head'd defenestrate

Dorothea Lasky

SONNET 60

The water turns my hands and I go into another nightmare

As the water turns into my hands, I go into another nightmare
So do these things that are gentle at their end
Each bending word with witches
In tender coil, all here, to do the others' discontent
For an infant devil, born upon this purple night
Right out of my head, his tiny horns I did not birth
But pulled his baby body from my eyes
Before the horns I gently loosened from my teeth
And the crown of Time that you made did I wear upon my head
And give to him, my other son
When you were young, I held you softly, too
But now your body, skin flush with vines
Is too monumental for my touch
So instead I throw you my words, praising thy unending worth

Uljana Wolf

SONNET 61

(who's watching)

what is wakefulness in translation? spaces between words: not a blink, but clouds in the shape of sheep. count them. in german, tired eyelids are kept open with matches. a gap and they stick to it. with or without their red heads? certainly, a glow. a stick-up for sleep. and when, in this deep light, you rub against each word, tossing and turning, you will find meanings shifting their shapes every minute—*shadows like to thee*, mocking, ungraspable. translation is this lament: you are so far from me—transformed into a sustained and reversed lullaby. do you watch clouds change their shape, or do you, by watching, change them? minutes grow into hours, hours into a wake. not over a dead body, but over one that is so alive as to be constantly absent, slipping away—*far off, with others all too near*. being awake in translation means to trace this distance, but never close the gap (eye, mouth), to keep alive the presence of the absent other and at the same time unmask one's own desire to merge with it, to finally meet one's match. in the space between the distant lovers (languages), this process unfolds as a shift from passive to active mode, a shadow play of failure and empowerment. first i am kept awake by the ghost of your language, then my language feels alive and awake because it watches yours—thereby creating its own images and slumber-breaking spirits. thus one could lament that 'to watch' also means to look intensly and/or wait in english, and that in german you'd wait for those meanings forever. but one could also point out that in german, unlike english, the words for being awake and keeping watch still show their common origin by sharing the exact same shape—*wach* and *Wache halten*—suggesting, perhaps, that being awake is not simply a state but the process of being constantly alert, of being watched by others and transgressing their watch at the same time. that it is in fact—like translation—a complicated collaborative process rather than a state or the result of not sleeping. gemeinsam wachsam—or else, *idle hours*. what, then, is a watchman in translation? she's someone who lets the sheep slip past the matches. a shepherd of *defeat* who intimately knows their desire to always be where *the others* are, and who also knows that, if they ever arrived at this distant, imagined place which slightly resembles Benjamin's *Ursprache*, language would stop wanting, waking and watching altogether, it would simply fall asleep.

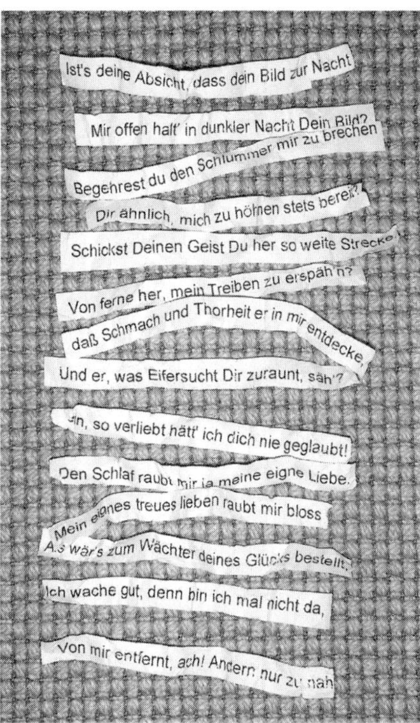

Is it your aim that at night your image
Markus Marti ca. 2009

Keeps open your image in the dark night?
Ferdinand Adolph Gelbcke 1867

Do you desire to rupture my slumber—
Gottlob Regis 1836

Alike thee, and ready to ridicule me?
Alexander Neidhardt 1870

Do you send your ghost such a long way,
Fritz Krauss 1872

from far away, to spy on what I do?
Emil Wagner 1840

that infamy and folly he shall find in me
Fritz Krauss 1872

And will, what jealousy breathes to you, see?
Ferdinand Adolph Gelbcke 1867

No, I never thought you to be so in love!
Markus Marti ca. 2009

My sleep is robbed but by my own love
Christia Schuenke 1994

my own true loving simply robs from me
Stefan George 1909

As if I were designed to be the watchman of your bliss
Terese Robinson 1927

I'm good at watching, cos in case I am not here,
Markus Marti ca. 2009

Afar from me, oh! too close to others everywhere.
Ferdinand Adolph Gelbcke 1867

Kate Greenstreet

SONNET 62

My father used to wear these shirts.

And I wore his
when he got new ones.

Did he realize he was getting fat? Am I like him?

How can I not

appreciate a sonnet
written by SHAKESPEARE. (Somehow I hit the caps lock.)

My lack of costume
is a costume itself.

Maybe I can't help seeing you in everything.

Elizabeth Willis — SONNET 63

Against love's battle lies: ungrammatical.
Inevitable meadow. A future tensed of all its past.

So time may take this beauty down
but beauty will fight itself to death.

The vampire day, top-heavy, white.
Erase, erased, erasing.

Aggrieved belief. He was my east and west.
He bound my breasts, I cut his hair.

I lay my words upon his mouth,
my mouth upon I cannot say.

All of grace is not device. Love
loves its past but not its thief.

May all its punishments remain untamed
upon this green unsentencing.

Cate Marvin

SONNET 63

Five ulcers I can name, five atomic springs
that call my belly's acids out for him whose
eyes are green as greenbacks, of whom I've
become too fond. Naïve, on thinking green,
I thought *spring*, offal. Awful, he's pulsing
in and out of range, does not return a ring,
lolls his loneliest dream, snuffles his breath
sweet against the luxurious thousand thread
count ply that crafts the exquisite soft of his
sheets. I lay there once. I'm lying to myself
right now. How could he read my letters if
he knows nothing but numbers? His brow,
crooked as a clock. He cannot see the bird.
He drives a car that crushes the bird, smiles
sailing his flashing vehicle down streams of
highway, for his future is sure, the number
is the mean. Clutch your gut: he's pulsing
in the ink. Love's finite, his murder means.

Thom Donovan

SONNET 64

Derek Beaulieu

SONNET 65

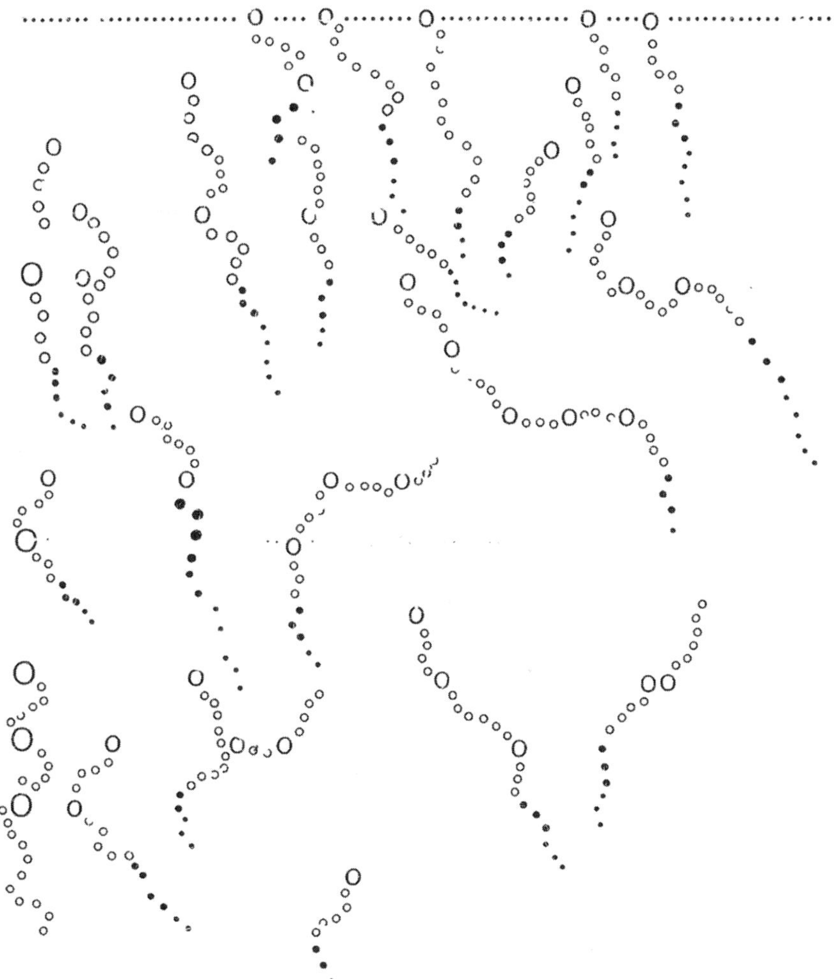

Janaka Stucky

SONNET 66

The world pisses on itself and takes
A million forms

The way winter melts and reminds
Us we're alone

Each drop of water punctuating
Our open mouths

Broken by absence but more
Beautiful for it

I want to be a part of all
Things I am apart of

Weave my nest from the teeth
Of laughter

And place it like a crown
Upon your departure's giant brow

I am less
Than an insect moving

From judgment to awe in all things

I am dust
On a moth

The whole universe
Printed on the wings of a moth

Mark Leidner

SONNET 67

well, this guy who doesn't suck is about to die
which double-sucks b/c he used to be amazing
and now a bunch of doom gets to haunt his body?
and interact with people on his behalf?
that's not fair, that isn't who he really is
he's more like he was before he got fucked
I don't understand why mister amazingness has to pretend
to be all about to die, fearing everything, etc
he should get doom back by killing himself
deny it the pleasure if it's getting to live vicariously
the more he lives, the more doom gets to?
doom wants to rub its greatness in our faces
b/c he was a massive bad-ass back in the day
so let's remember him as he seemed that way

Brenda Hillman

SONNET 68

The Nets Between Solstice & Equinox

[. . . golden tresses of the dead. . .
—Shakespeare, Sonnet 68

—& the wren can see us
from its canister of loud joy but we cannot
see it. Often a particle of chaos passes
& we barely notice in the summer air.
The baby is running; he clings
to his cardboard cow. Baseball trading, the debt
ceiling parts like the Astrodome, to the sky;
Congress teeters, the right wing swells;
the left wing withers till the body cannot fly.

In the woods, the lichen falls quietly,
half-algae, half-fungus like poetry. (Today
it resembles that death-is-the-brother-
of-beauty netting on the mouths
of America's secret army). Should
every nature talk to each other?
Shakespeare marvels at his friend's wig,
made from a dead person's hair…

Nerve's work, where is thy energy?
You're tired, even at dawn. From the *peep peep*
nppp, hops through fog's wispy pre-writing
  in the oak. Clump-clump-clump.
Your love is getting breakfast by himself.
For thou hast given us thy absence.
  —*Why are you talking like that?*
  —*So i can escape from the net the net*
   & dance with the dancing fleas

Nathaniel Otting & Kelin Loe SONNET 69

BITS OF SONNET ATTENTION OVER THE WALL

Those separates of you are smarting. Sex is mine is the one that exits the sonnets. What paragraphs is when no breaks for the eye means less reading it means you hide inside your human. The world sees everything but what you just in case erase or the same world reverses praise when you show your other ways like when you, say, go make a lake. What I get is green if we can't company. After before the flowers of friendship faded friendship faded but before the flowers of bad is that summer was so gross. Gone agley. What non : sonnet :: not : wolf. His famous flower called him famous flower. The distance between scale and method just got different than a certain thing. Objects provide the world with the center of a flower the lodger is solving an oh no prospect of a flower the lodger is lacking. That what is made by more of your inner, permitted thinking of what's most excellent. The very *of* of the mouth of a mammal of relation of subject of action of immaterial of part. A new lows you. In circles we go night and we're consumed firely by what purgatory O Book circulating simple constancy. Covers so flat extent opponents remember some kindly. Your away consequence with away activase are an aureole for all that plural identical hunting cry that entires you private. Sonnet avoidance til some effed sonnet snuck up on the midbrain. Dura alternative marks of nature-nature and we are activase and we are defeated by others wisely. Some mayor was all type out the greatest sonnets or other sooner flower the worst book ever soiled either we wrote it that bad our selves didn't or it went and got bent rotten. Thy diamond is just a word paragraph you mean another sonnet. When you soil your flower you've gots to leave your warden permission to call gods in her cell in the middle of reading this world. Flowers maintains it figures that a book drowns in berries. Writers paint they don't speak and would paint something and Jean-Michel would paint over it. Marlowe would. That sonnet went to begin an attention language outside an actual volume: Freon-Hölderlin. This and non-this had touched each other nearly to life. How names got in here. By dint of declares a seat of dignity more remote an element seconds comparison a verb of pheasants sends postcards from a nude person singular. ~~Unspecified sex expresses the direction of the intended object encloses the combined perfection of form and charm and scale and measure and value: lunula memory. As well as those, present conjecture, the unspecified abstemizes by your waste material from an excavation. Afterward/afterward, a man simply, the heeding function of being human does not withstand the fact that the unspecified colors of the iris exist origin. Motion in the direction your gathering of buyers and sellers flow-gate; join greater the disease of birds sniff; this indicates the thing; a sudden febrile attack. Introduce contrast: hence often expressing protest. So your sanctity ointment fumigating casks by burning sulfur sticks short [substitute for a negative clause] your manifest exhibit. The miry or muddy place used by a wild boar for wallows in happens close at hand. Observed by me in the singular~~ present, the body free of very fortress evolves a forms a free burgher. The capital profits that which a man has in the land or waters of another hunger. The beginning of vegetable life grains corn from the sheaf as from a germ happens to hey that wilds next to us. You second person. A wave what fastens these are my investigations. The wonders they happened of a sudden come unsung that before I knock I need to know who's there. If my beloved even begins to call I'm all like I'm ears that I'm not so fun I'm sure. These are investigations of what never works. Who kept up all nights super wondering where everyone's pinkest dream. Out of outs! The world ends in a frosty. My eyes played me. Motion gets in you and you go.

Cyrus Console — SONNET **XXL**

Whispers do not make you less beautiful
Whispers are side effects of beautiful
The odd canker sore spices up oral
One crow's foot says chill; the face is mortal

When you take really great care of yourself
Whispers broadcast how great you look and feel
At 35 or so for example
Way, way, way better than the typical

Uh, child actor, child soldier, child model
You really turned out incredibly well
Great skin & hair, awesome job, great dental
And something else unparaphrasable

If you were perfect, you'd be an a-hole
Pure class isn't really classy at all

Pierre Joris

SONNET 71

Shakespeare's sonnet #71, re-Englished after Paul Celan's German version without consulting the original even once:

You should, once I'm gone, mourn only as long
as you hear the bell, the dark one, from the tower;
as long as it needs to tell the world:
He who lived with you went to live with the worms.

This I write, but you, having read it,
forget who wrote it. For look—I love you:
I wish I'd never been on your mind,
for when you think of me, sorrow steals upon you.

You should let—once your gaze rests upon these words,
once I'm dust, dust & no longer—
love become what I became,
and my name, do not speak it again:

The world, wise-eyed, already looks for your tears,
me, now gone, with you to taunt.

Noelle Kocot

SONNET 72

Reverence is Ours

Heaven in a ditch, the circle of little angels.
The future is a wound, the dissonant rev
Of whirling sentences. Your falsetto is alive
In these woodland wells, and this shine

Is more tribal melody than instrument.
Oh, you who have a watery sympathy with
Dirt, oh you mud and sticks and crawly
Things, the room is wandering on its depths,

You live in a flock of time, alive in that mirror.
The silence of the day is for exploring,
And your fever is an object. What do you have?
Stay home and smoke pipes. The whole continent

Is being tugged at. When did it last rain?
The lane is ending and there are no signs.

Calvin Bedient

Everything Suck Big Suck Big Six Buttons

(after Shakespeare's Sonnet 73 and Hans Arp's "I Am a Horse")

The squid writing Cloud-Pump on the clouds
wait to fall down women's blouses.
They wriggle their roots above my 3-watt
nipples are their flashlights when the night is blue.

But I am through with bleating at the berrygates.
Paint a cherry if you want the milk of love.

A bare ash Venus scatters now   everything
my sack of twigs. I have had it   suck
with material   big
girls and boys, 73   suck
rolling around on a bed, fat Uccello horses,   big
they have *none* of the Qualities, just swells,
ouch, reddenings, "*love* that." They're poor
like *that*, they love that.

Who will pet the tiger throws
on industry leaders knees? Upon whose airs   seals
will I rise, a shimmering chord of exquisitivity   bark
sharked from the meat-holes in the choir's faces,   in
females to the virile smell of burning money?   the
Snow that fell arrest early this marmalade.   choir

Branches snap in the west's yellow back. meat-
I flick off the 73 maggots of the old. holes
Lean on me, moment, lubricate the major organs.
Can I still spit on the red square and the blue?

Next to the tree frogs singing near the sky,
it's you I love, my Kilimanjaro pad,
your Eden skin, your axis knees. paint
And after that the little sparrows of the fire. a
cherry

Katharina Grosse's Styrofoam Sidney Opera
House sorts of icebergs squeal squeakily
in the quiet where late the calves
consumed considerable attention ("numerous publications")
milk
among heaps of rainbow-popsicle dirt. of
(What a gross substance, Styrofoam. Cruushhh it. Try!) love
Painting is such fire! I have painted the fur
wind arriving with the sleet

of everybody's autobiography. But for you,
Mother Fish, I make my delicatest drawings
in a boat floating over your cold ardor
where the bones have no harbor.

Here is a turquoise fly, still wet, take it;
and here a coral twig, a tiny hair of the sea.

Brandon Brown

SONNET **74**

Hi To Antonio Gramsci In Hell

I'm so mad at T.I. right now!
The ignominy of his arrest, community service,
windshield praxis against the juridical sun.
Allergic to snitching as child to peanut. I waited months
like dust for his parole, and then he boards
a fucking party bus to the halfway house and goes right
back in the cage? Clank clank go the doors encrypting
one of the world's greatest artists.
Can you see me?
I mean, can you see the real me underneath
the blood and bow tie? The me mad
at T.I., mad at the sovereign architects
of these prisons. The real me who eats peanuts
when my pockets go elephantine. Unfurled grumpy glottal stop of gold
puke. Glitter puke shot from a phallic cannon and into
the mouth of my beloved / supervisor.
Remember that one time I tried to sell my soul but nobody
tipped my bell? The sinews chewed all the way through.
Halfway house welcome party deflated like a flag on September 11th…
Unscorched purple. Dregs of beer fortify remorse
of a sad and outraged heart, bitter at the sonnet-strict
bureaucracy which cages kings. If I was about to be guillotined
I'd probably think "oops!?" What would you think?
I am so sick of being so mad at a form of life
that abuses paisley transmission. Put me back on any party bus whatsoever.
Bail me as the lips of fish unfurl a poetics of non-wriggling.
A king's carelessness burns me, but how am I going to burn it back?

You're not going to starve Picasso. Fries cost four dollars. The sheen
of iron kissing plastic between my lips and the lips of TIP
immeasurable hoard of fantasy treasure. It makes sense to want
to kiss a cage but do you always have to marry what you love?

Kelli Anne Noftle

SONNET 75

brain in belly
yes, thoughts

salted pavement
spring drain
called evergreen

a little piece

to covet
(you are not a robot)

between us between
distance in km

moment by minute

the clapping

get on my hands and knees

guess you could say

god made
the question

through man

made red the sky

reads Oh— (I just like to speak)

sometime, at
times
worms either…

you waste
or/
way
was was

starve over
abundant no,
not by far

excess uh huh in

feeding dogs
dog food

what proof is (do I have to keep)

too little

Joseph Bradshaw

SONNET **76**

Larry Edison Bradshaw was my teenage lover.
Bethany Wright was my huswife lover.
God be gracious to all nighttime lovers.
I call each of them my own Paul Thek.

Why do these names bear weight I can't carry.
Each of these names contains a barren bird.
Barren, it carries the name forward.
What I write I can't carry.

Oppen: What I couldn't write I scratched out.
Oppen: What I couldn't write I call "bird."
George Oppen: the last Romantic poet.
George Oppen is my father and also my lover.

I wrote this sonnet while watching my father die.
I was lost inside him, his cunt's name was Larry.
I was lost inside him and I bear his name true.
When my father died I called him my true lover.

True Larry in the dark, he felt just like Bethany.
In the Book of the Father this is rendered as Oppen, fucking his dead mother,
crying out
to his wife Mary I thought you were her back pressed against my belly.

Sophos.com
Sysinternals
Wikipedia

DukeUniversityBasketball.Net
WePlayTheGame.com
UntilTheFatLadySings.com

ProsperousWoman.com
UnbelievableDiscounts.com
ShipVia.Us

Deliri.us
FlashbackToTheSixties.com
FireBrickRed.com

NoiseDecibels.com
SoundDecibels.com

Emily Pettit

SONNET 77

Your sand shows and shows a castle collapsing.

You bring your finger around and around.

Absent ideas impress upon an area in mind.

Here's this look, with your head astound, astound.

The folds for seeing your sand, as it goes through

your hand. Mouths call and call back, give and take

memory. You around and around and somewhere

knowing, a cunning continuum counting as it can

and can. See some memory. Miss some too. Hold it.

Have it. Let it go. Tell the blank it is an opportunity.

It is a bank. By a bank you have a brain and you

brain. Taking to new time and ways to take time.

These spaces of time, it took. It took telling a book.

Look book, you bank you branch. You book. See sand.

Claire Donato

SONNET **78**

So: A Baroque

To raise a family, an academic structure, in an environment made
up of walls does not interest us. 'When the baby is born, there is no
place to put it,' Laura Riding said, now do you know what this says
about me. Was feeling under the weather, woke a little
nervous, if you love it you can keep it, yet in retrospect jettisoned
employment, marriage, and/or nostalgia is too much, the slur
abysmal not enough, 'I do hope you find everything you need,' but what
if this heady Surreality provides me with a sense of self
sustaining community? So oft have I invoked these words in other works
to speak to thee, little green whose multilingual tongue 'aye' catches fruit
less lodestar, dumb & unexcused from class to spite the common
good. Therefore, in vitro, one is not bold. But thou art
all my thoughts on walks these days.
In a fugue, think it over, make space.

Jordan Davis

SONNET 79

I can see why you might have asked
Another poet to send you lines—
Only so many times a man can stand
To be told he'd better have a baby.

And I've said it before I'll say it
As often as I forget it hasn't worked yet—
You're the lost original of a million poems.
But this guy, really?

You both draw breath, him mostly hot wind;
You're best and superlatives
Are his once and future nourishment;
You wear clothes, he cuts language by the yard.

Come see your tailor, put those things back on the rack;
If I have to read him, you'll find me dressed in black.

Julie Doxsee

SONNET 80

How do I write a word that says I suffocate
knowing a buffed spirit stalks you, abuses your
sacrifice to torque his one-track muscle
that shuts me up with the yap yap yap.
You know your wet goes coast to coast—
or do you? Your sheen of white waits
to catch the wind (him) and dampen
from the surface a loud scream (me). Just
give me, please, a skin-touch or something.
While he goes to the pin-drop infinity inside you
I dry out outside—smashed, splintered, shrunk.
He is a confident skyscraper and super hot.
If you choose his bulk over my saucy bark
it is my fault only; this love illness kills me.

Jeremy Schmall

SONNET 81

You have your doubts.
I can tell from the furrow
in your forehead & the placement
of your handgun, in this basement
apartment/office where the sinners,
if it is their sincere desire,
may repent between the hours
of 7:30 a.m. and 6:30 p.m.
The news anchor's face is flattened
against the smooth hide
of "advanced RCA technology"
atop the mini fridge.
Everything is okay, I speak
to myself in the little bathroom
staring at a mirror spotted with toothpaste
and saliva beside a handwritten note
taped to linoleum detailing careful instruction
on using the silver flushing
mechanism, which to my horror
I now hold in my outstretched
arm when I return to the party,
calling it a party, though it's more
a collection of belt buckles and men
with certain gestures
and clear ownership of a beverage table.
The format is simple.
It's a simple format. Like the cockpit
of a silver automobile.
The one whose radio dims

when I press the pedal,
and inside from which
the lake unspooled "on the starboard
side," you'd said. I had been thinking
just then how 'afternoon' is like a room,
the bad room with the papasan
and small lamp on the floor.
You bounced in the seat beside me,
an object of enthusiasm. My mouth,
which is the ventilation point
for the body's dark mechanisms,
what did my mouth do—

Caroline Bergvall

SONNET 82

You're

So

Cool

You

Don't

Need

Poetry.

Sure.

Tho

Check'it,

Mine

Hits

Thine

Spot.

Ish Klein

SONNET 83

Today the sun died at one twenty five.
Chimes in the future in dreams in the future.
It is not beautiful to be alone.
And I am not alone. You are with me.
Good reality is a strength habit.
Our house is good though dies when we leave it.
My name is erased: chalk off the pavement.
But the names you say stand up from the grave.
What good is praise? What good is a name?
My body cycles a place in a way.
It was a job, it is a job. I do
work. This planet equally weighted
by five grave futures names alone do create. Pavement
habit you call it as you lift me away from it.

Laura Mullen

SONNET 84

Fonond

Mmosst iss itt ssays whwho thatt whwhich ssay mmore can
Prraisse thiss rrich ththat ththann arre youyou youyou alonne
Inn thethe sstore immured iss thethe whosse confinned
Should whwhich whwherre equal yourr example grrew
Withinn pennury leann ththat ddothth penn ddwell
Ssome ssubject tto glory his ssmall nnott thatt lenndss
Ttell if hehe can thatt writtes hehe of you butt
Ssttory hiss dignifiess are thatt sso youyou youyou
Butt lett you whatt is in him copy writt
Mmaking clearr nnot wwhat wworsse mmade nnaturre sso
Ssuch counterpartt fame sshall a witt hiss and
Everry admmirred hiss sstyle mmaking wherre
Bblessings youyou bbeauteouus too add a youyourr currse
Praisespraise onon praisepraise wwhich makes beinng yourr
wworrse

Kate Durbin

SONNET 85

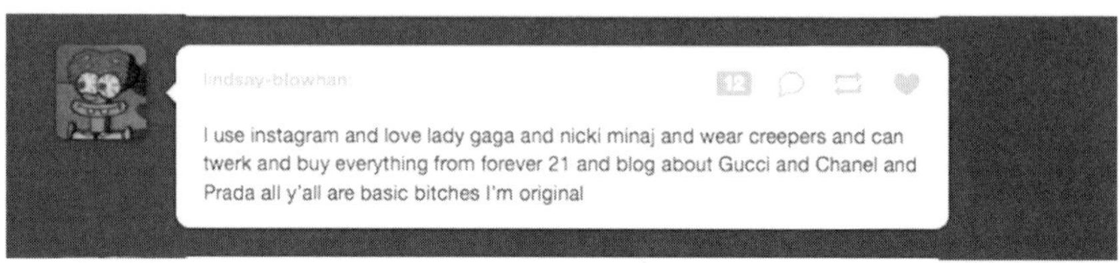

Sina Queyras

SONNET 85

My **tongue**-tied **Muse** in manners holds her still,
While comments of your **praise** richly compiled,
Reserve thy character with golden **quill**,
And precious **phrase** by all the Muses filed.
I think good thoughts, whilst others write good words,
And like unlettered clerk still cry 'Amen'
To every hymn that able spirit affords,
In polished form of well-refined pen.
Hearing you praised, I say *tis so, 'tis true,'*
And to the most of praise add something more;
But that is in my thought, whose love to you,
Though words come hindmost, holds his rank before.
Then others, for the breath of words respect,
Me for my dumb thoughts, speaking in effect.

Effect in speaking, thoughts dumb ~~my~~ for me
Respect words or breadth ~~the~~ for, others ~~then~~
Before rank ~~his~~ holds, hindmost come ~~words through~~
You to love whose thought ~~my in~~ is that but
More something add praise of most   to and
'true tis,' so tis, say I, praised ~~you hearing~~
pen refined-well, ~~of~~ form ~~polished in~~,
affords spirit ~~able~~ that hymn ~~every~~ to
Amen' cry still clerk unlettered ~~like~~ and
Words, ~~good~~ write, others whilst ~~thoughts~~ good think I
Filed muses ~~the all by~~ phrase precious and
Quill golden ~~with character~~ thy reserve
Compiled richly praise your ~~of~~ comments ~~while~~
Still ~~her~~ holds manners in muse tied-tongue ~~my~~.

Effect in speaking, thoughts dumb for me
Respect words or breadth for, others
Before rank holds, hindmost come
You to love whose thought is that but
More something add praise of most to and
'true tis,' so tis, say I, praised
pen refined-well, form ,
affords spirit that hymn
Amen' cry still clerk unlettered and
Words, write, others whilst good think I
Filed muses phrase precious and
Quill golden thy reserve
Compiled richly your comments
Still holds manners in muse tied-tongue

Final Version

Tied-tongue muse in manners holds still
Comments, your richly compiled reserve
Thy quill qolden
And precious phrase muses, filed
I think good, whilst others write words
(unlettered clerk still cry amen) that
hymn spirit affords
form well-refined pen praised
I, say tis so tis true to (and)
Most of praise add something more
That is thought whose love to you
Come hindmost, holds rank before
Others for breadth, or words, respect me
For dumb thoughts, speaking in effect.

John Coletti

SONNET 86

Kissed never
kissed   always kissing
baroque at an arm's length
Paul Smith
denied light
two amber hairs
11th rib / the lash
God's bones
beside Jacksonville
no trace all yr sweater

Lawrence Giffin

SONNET 87

Free porn! thou art too dear for my possessing.
I like " 'you' with your little tail of vowels,"
and "I prefer 'you' in the plural."
Tête full of theory *sans* New Haven bachelor,
pumping my machine like some wage-slave
silent and compliant. *Das Kapital!* My Capital!
You were my clear pleasure, my dear surplus.
Given up before we got off, two Tallies in one,
co-eds in florid heat, at the mall down from Stone's
tallywhacker and coinpurse, tower of civic power,
buying me flesh-colored Levi's.
You were my Baudelairean heritance, my Hölderlinian
pension. Wasted on your off-campus dorm floor
at your double oughts under a blanket we still cover
a cat-clawed couch arm with.
Just now, my wife was like, "Remember when we melted
a strainer trying to make weed butter?" She was harkening back
to our honeymoon sampling thawed Tex-Mex in cell-patchy Appalachia.
I did remember, and her mischievousness was uncharacteristic,
like the lid was taken off it for the first time in years.
All the sudden, she was herself again—more but also more corruptible.

An argument in *Cosmo*:
Is your lover fortuitous and inexplicable or
groundless and unreasonable?
The poetry lover buys his own troth, cash and carry,
for that one love, one life, owed
to God, sputtering hearse-speak in costly OP.
I go to White Cube and look at all the stuff.

Now I can only hear, "Wet dreams may come."
The Reagan-bound plane banked and
fell a hundred points.
The stewardess gave us passengers lids and straws
for our cups of wine.
Impulsive. O Captain! My *Kharon!*
Upright in my seat right up until deplaning,
and again when upon sight of you in baggage claim
I came to—ah, there's the rub! You
in your Ally Sheedy Georgetown pearls,
no casket but carpet burn.
And I in my cap. It all, didn't we almost have?
Anyone can see for themselves that McCarthy can't kiss
on screen or off (do tell!), he just goes "puh, puh, puh"
in pretty girls' mouths.
And though I always fancied myself a duck man,
I'm rather more tooth-sweet like Blane or Kevin Dolenz—incisive.

I walked with them up to the Pinch District and tried some oysters,
but I already knew it was too late for me and turned toward other pleasures,
those few that wouldn't arrive for months, years even.
I was like a preposition. I brushed up against what was
there just to see, but I never stayed long. The slightest nudge and it starts
its apology. The others were starting to move on
to the next ember on the street half-paved with stones,
but I wanted to have
nowhere I needed to be. To not have to need or need to be.
To turn one's face like a giant placard to the parking forests
of Camden. To sound my "O.K." up the rainspouts and over the unused tram
tracks of Poplar or Main empty and hazy with boxwoods.
I did not know then that all that time I was swerving toward you.
A life is just the sum of its disappointments (that came out all wrong),

absently piled like salt spilled on the counter.
Still it adds up and is carried over by another operation I was
forever too distracted to learn. Only
a handful of possibilities, really, from which I always picked just one.
You reached down for your purse but found me instead,
which made it hard for you to buy the things you wanted to own.
You had to start taking them, and what you couldn't take I didn't want to give you.
It might as well be yours, since you already own it.

O Prada-clad daughter, when will you cease your slumming and return
to the O.C., knowing full well how well you fare
in this loose-fitting globe? When will you loafe and invite *my* Soul?
I just start Googling stuff. So when "SmokeBluntz" pops up
on your Caller ID, you'll know it's me, bringing you back from Summer Waves,
and up onto Looking Glass Rock where the trail opens up on the chalky bald.
We just sort of stare out at it, all that stuff that just is, out there, each
releasing any claims to the other. And then we carry it between us
like an invisible thing that we carry between us.

Trisha Low

SONNET 88

Just read me and see if this number is not full of good things.

PET SUPERSTITIONS ... Page 14
(He hounded himself into a raging feud..)

Anxiety Warrant #1 is rarely used: "Nothing."

Anxiety Warrant #2 is self-explanatory: "*Something* is!" he insisted.

Anxiety Warrant #1 is rarely used: A blinding rage fired her blood. She smashed her fist on the table, upsetting a wine glass, the red liquid spattering the linoleum on the floor. "It was me that found Minelli! It was me that led the dicks to where Minelli was!

Anxiety Warrant #2 is self-explanatory: You belong to me! Me! I turned Minelli in for you! You understand?"

Anxiety Warrant #3 has no ambivalence: Her voice was shrill and loud but her eyes beseeched him to hear her plea.

Anxiety Warrant #4 is a good example: The papers were not telling the truth about her. The papers, too, had been hoodwinked. They were all conspiring. "They're trying to screw me out of you,"

Anxiety Warrant #3 has no ambivalence: he cried bitterly, his face contorted with pain. "I knew something was fishy when you tried giving me the brushoff. But I went along to the station house to put in my claim. They said to beat it or they'd lock me up for disturbing the peace. I lost my head.

Anxiety Warrant #4 is a good example: I punched one of 'em. Tossed you out …" She licked her dry lips: "I went to the papers and told 'em the story. I just came from there now …" He shook his head as if trying to awaken her faltering memory. "We'll see who gets you! Just watch the papers tomorrow morning …" Then

Anxiety Warrant #5 is a very high place: she raised her powerful hands and wrung them, her gaze directed at the ceiling, as if there lay the explanation.

Anxiety Warrant #5 is very high place: The calamity that had befallen him. "Why was it done?" she thought. "What made him do it?"

Ai Madonna. Fierce, shameless love would be a mirror and no shield.

Erín Moure — SONNET 89

SANGLANT '89, translated from an unadmitted language

I am tired of the diarrhea rhetoric, OK you throw it off and it lands again as demogogy in embroidered shirts. No one wants my memorial pain, OK! Caught between two enemas and a friend, the library where all the zombies I had unearthed had given way but other perverts of delirium still emerge. When I think of memory, OK I break its head. Stooped farmers torched by Tourettes still weather crops while wives stir stoves and distances. Bow to the pop songsters! Like me on Facebook! Pop pills! I still don't know why I was fried OK, by paranoids playing pinball with their blemish trollops. Undigested blurbs of redigerate vomiting and arguments, OK what use are arguments to those who sacrificed for their country and a country is a palimpsest *merde* on *merde*. I am going to die from my face, OK. And bleat from an orifice! I am going to die from my arm, OK and from my jointed elbow and I am going to die from my facial skin. I can't die from what's below, not from bone ground into cinders, not from squirming earth, OK and I won't die yet from your neuralgia!

Stan Apps

SONNET 90

A general disdain drools in my ocean.
All of them hate me, and why the hell not?
What am I to them, or they to I
That they shouldn't spit in my eye?
As for you, we all like to hear the worst:
It gives us a chance to get ready and stay
Well away from the fucked-in-the-head ones.
So I'll just assume you hate me the same
As the people who have every reason to,
And by every reason I mean
Plenty of other fish in the sea,
Why risk biting into the wrong red berry.
There are so many chances to not connect
It would make no sense to value one.

Bhanu Kapil

SONNET 91: an excerpt:

Thy love is better than high birth to me,
Richer than wealth, prouder than garments' cost,
Of more delight than hawks or horses be;
And having thee, of all men's pride I boast:
  Wretched in this alone, that thou mayst take
  All this away and me most wretched make.

SONNET 91: the last two lines:

All day, fierce bits of feeling. And magic. Napping, I'm woken by a bird singing so loudly and at such a strange time of day, I physically get out of my bed and leave the house. But it's just birdsong and not an emergency of some kind. I stand in the garden in my nightgown listening to one bird singing desperately to another bird, who doesn't sing back, but merely bounces from branch to branch in the ragged tree between my house and the neighbors', and understand: it's Spring.

HOW FRAGMENTS ATTRACT: Ecstatic pilgrimage, dismemberment, and the recombinant text.

In writing about bodies on the point of, or just after, dispersal: what happens to the parts of the body just before they touch the ground? These are notes towards a diasporic or immigrant poetics, with a closer look at non-Western models of recombinance and futurity. How can experimental writing bring an attentive, ritual approach—an adequate form—to the question of bodies and violence? And at the moment that the body "reappears"—in time—in a different form—

how might a "recombinant text" avoid the fantasy of re-integration? In my writing, I want to think about fragments. I want to think about a fragment as vibration: as both sound and light.

I wrote these sentences in the aftermath of a relationship with a poet that left me so wretched that, hearing birdsong, I reacted with the full force of my brain. I left the house, ragged. Just as I opened my beak, ragged, to him: in an earlier time. I think it is possible to survive the last line of Sonnet 91; the only way is to plunge into writing like a hawk, or horse, loosened from its dynamic tether. In the time that followed the breakdown of a great love, I made a pilgrimage to the Ganges and analyzed fragments like the devotee that I was: an adjunct pleasure (writing) that was forced into a primary position. (The source of all delight.) But these particulars are not my measure.

I was born beneath a cedar tree, at ten in the morning, in a London summer that brightened then darkened in turns.

Jonathan Skinner

SONNET 92

Go ahead, steal away:
You're mine for life.
Life won't outlast love,
It hinges on your love.
No need to fear the worst
When the least ends my life.
I've better things in store
Than your smile can stay.
Your moods won't vex me,
Since your revolt kills me.
What a happy title,
In love, happy to die!
But who's above suspicion?
Are you cheating on me?

Christopher Schmidt

SONNET 93

Word

a safe word only works if you can remember it
a memory is only a memory if you first forget it
punishing each other for not writing more poetry
we doubled up sex and lyric for efficiency
a master-teacher suggested palinodes, which suited us
so we devised constraints, making us chattier
we bought masks, forcing us to use our hands for signing
bought hands (four) to conserve our own for transcribing
we grew apart, not for the usual reasons
for semaphore. Through translating we lost weight
we looked great which measuring the distance
was torture. Nietzsche: a split self enjoys dominating *and*
submitting. Poetry is divided? As this poem
I can't remember the safe word —stop, no —erase.

Safe

Supposing true
like husband
altered me
place heart in
live hatred
cannot therefore change
looks heart's
frowns writ
heaven decree but
ever face
thoughts heart's
nothing but
like Eve's apple doth grow
If not virtue answer

kathryn l. pringle

SONNET 94

that one overarching, yet unreaching
may not wound though breathing
so still, they lie
an unmoving state conceiving foul:
feigned injury on a field
the flower of that venerated paradise
no evidence remains upon its face
still grows rich and larger
and still to itself is just
itself. a fleeting representative of summer
but watchers of such capital, do recall
one representative
left in the sun too long
is rancid perfume in the end

Andrew Joron

SONNET 95

A: all, an And.

Beauty, beauty's blesses
blot budding
but

can canker, cannot
chose comments.
Cover

days, dear dispraise,
Dost doth

edge, enclose, every
eyes.

Fair for fragrant—
Got habitation?

Hardest, have heart,
heed his, how ill,
ill-used in kind.

Knife, large, lascivious like,
lose lovely make.

Making mansion name,
naming O! O!

Of on/out:
praise privilege,
report rose,
see shame, sins, sport—

Spot story,
sweet sweets,

Take tells that,
the thee, their things—

This those,
thou,

thy, to
tongue
turns veil—

Vices: what, where, which—

Ben Estes

SONNET 96

By no fault of yours you are young
young man. August and yappy
your yapping's a regalness to my heart sung
loudly, and with confidence, comely.
Your practiced misshapen charms
can charm the glare from silver,
and since the silver charms always appear unharmed
your crew'll never question your glamor.
How many other men have you led off course
with false tales of back-alleys and roof-tops?
None, for I know with tender remorse
the marks on your sheets are but tear-drops.
I love you child, for being able to unsheathe
the pearly underside you keep hidden, down beneath.

Chris Martin

SONNET 97

Almas

It isn't winter, exactly. Since you've gone it's like it is, but instead of snow we're drowning under little fluttering tufts of ash drawn down the throat of anyone trying to escape. As if we could. Glazed gray daylight and pawed eyeholes just to see. Which is fine, really, I could be blind and it wouldn't matter. If only it didn't feel so naked. Ash-tufted and buck at every block party. Human one-hitters. And it's not even September! We're *supposed* to be naked! Can you remember how it was last summer? Primitive, unstitched, bodies throbbing like biceps freed after months curled inside the Velcro hug of blood pressure. Now first thing each morning I pull on a white tourniquet of redundant briefs just to watch my thighs black out. And we aren't pregnant, exactly. It's like we are, but instead of bellies we have zeros, and these zeros just get rounder and rounder, not bearing anything, abiding not even the smallest blitz of fission or generosity one could call a product. I keep listening to the new Big K.R.I.T. mixtape, each inertial vowel sinking into the zero of my barrenness until I'm literally shoveling coffee into my hole and begging for swagger. Winter's still a line break cum enter button just waiting to get depressed, but my voice, I mean the rags my voice have become, are just stringy wattles getting sneezed at, like Zoidberg with a cold. An exposed viral pulse. So come back. Seriously. Even if it has to wait until school starts or Christmas break or j-term or whatever they're calling it these days. Even if it's the dead of winter and snow *really is* ash and we *really are* bargaining with god for some passage into flowers. I would take that. I would sing through soil if it came to that. Come back and I swear: it will all totally undie. I will summer. I will explode every zero like a load of Beluga between roof and tongue and I will do it until I puke summer. Almas even. Iranian diamonds. Exactly like I'm the Caspian Sea and we're pressurizing graphite in the vise of my mouth. Allotropes of carbon that burst into dwarf whales. That exact.

John Yau

SONNET 98

When spring is in knots
And proud Apron is spied
—dressed in all his scrim—
Heaving everything in the spit of youth,
Crowned with Saturnine laughter,
There is still the netherworld's sweet smell
Different floral fragrances and Ko's lore
Maybe the sun of following states
An empty lot is proud of its courage
I wonder why white is receiving compliments
On how deep red is in the earth's rising color;
She is not sweet, but my fingers of light:
Take you back, as will winter, and a face
With its shadow permanently removed

Ronaldo V. Wilson

SONNET 99

(Mis) translation A: Shakespeare's Love Sonnet #99

The forward violet thus did I chide:

At a repose, the tip of his hood peeled back to cock-rim, dots, perhaps violet, if that memory were a bluish purple, an end of the spectrum that opposes origin. Lost a watch in the Hyatt that morning, face broke. The part exposed could almost cut, so, too, like the flower ripped from root, it scolds. Incidentally, you're nothing like this: "Putanginamo" is where you'll search, *your mother was a whore*. Motherfucker in disgust, you're ripped from one language, cheeks pinched in by chicken-fat hands, a sponge stuffed in your mouth. The jets boom above the sonnet from which you're obviously distant, so far from the realm of flora. So delicate, the flower fronts: Namumulaklak, and here I am, my mind leaks, vision through a cord at the end of which a camera peeks. The "eye" sees through where the brain's been pierced—a gasket embedded in the skull that forever leaks.

Sweet thief, when didst thou steal thy sweet that smells,
If not from my love's breath?

Flora-hi-jacked, jinxed paralingual terror. He gestures to the flower—how did you steal that sweetness: *I'd take it all. I'd take it all. I'd run away*. As T.C. sings, sure, the project could be one of parallels, but you need to mark where one smells bagong on the fingers, from the fridge, then a taste, repelled, you slam it back into the rack. This is what they eat. This is what I eat. This is what I ate. It should be "*Tengo* hambre, mucho hambre." You literally "have hunger." I have a dream. I am dumb tongued, but seek your stolen breath, your first language, not even an accent, so you'll pass as anyone into everything.

My mistress' eyes in a swinger's paradise—two couples, both mounted and mounting, amateurs—really—I'm all mixed up. You're so confused, some would say, what breath did you endure to breathe as if that flower? My fingers smell like shit after shitting. And while eating, even after antibacterial gel, did I taste the bagong with the same?

Thy purple pride
Which on thy soft cheek for complexion dwells
In my love's veins thou hast too grossly dyed.

My impulse is to dig out from what I don't remember, a few words, here or there, curse words, are what they say when they can say nothing in a language lost. While I am simply stain, your beauty is light. Who are they that say we don't blush? What's in our realm? What kind of failure is it to say the veins in lines of purple track a beautiful body? And so he gives good face, but all I can recall is The American Super Nanny comforting black Nevada, whose brothers and sisters, also black, frame her, *you're dark.* If this were stable, say one for one and this for that, what body could hue a black-baby's-waterworks-at-Santa's-rejection. *Simultaneous*: This word my mother taught me early, and it wasn't in any language but the one I spoke, all my life, to abandon accent, *do I still HAB one now?* Her cheeks are pink in the pale of her skin, jawbones sunken into what's recalled, a flash recast in the missing. How do you say sunken-cheek, shadow, in Tagalog? les joues/ creuses/ hundido/ sunken-cheek/ hollow.

The lily I condemned for thy hand,

I can't resist the impulse to intrude my own clawing for language in the ease of this—Alert, Lily, and the hierarchy promulgates the vexed relationship between what's known, and what gets re-articulated, "lily-white"? Or is it the shape, the spread of my brown hand out of a taupe sweater, over the shoulder as it gets wider, my arm around his nylon black jacket, his shoulder over the memory of that peace lily in the hot car that shriveled in the heat, where only water and love brought it back to bloom, white, orange pollen powdered onto a thick leaf, so like his hand.

And buds of marjoram had stol'n thy hair:
The roses fearfully on thorns did stand,

Scent: all of it taken to understand the clean of this budded hair, Prelled, today. Lost in the fear of what's gone, the poem's turn, caught in another trail, led from stem to tip, through a road of thorns. My interlude: The dust under the couch is hand swept into grey piles, like the shit in the pot that doesn't get flushed, long before the walk is taken. This is the slowness of memory lost, of what waste promises, what gets trapped in the hair. Mi pelo: the rose is connected to another armature, breaking. Look closer to see the split ends.

One blushing shame, another white despair;
A third, nor red nor white, had stol'n of both

Somewhere between shame and despair, the flower steals the self. Description guilty plant, body swamped, like alligators shot in the back by rifle, or close-up, in the head, by pistol, in the water from long distances, the shooter, his teeth, gone, aims into the river. The quiet isn't needed for this TV murder, where bubbles expose position. When I asked if there was a word for sunken cheeks, *yes, there's a word for that*, but said she'd be sleeping when I got back. So distant the connection between languages, agency, how we taught them both French and German at home, and he learned English in school—It's a shame your mother didn't teach you her language. Where flowers take the face, what then does language do to retrieve, mistranslation, un-document, the impossible?

And to his robbery had annex'd thy breath;

Gun-flower. How to name this occasion, find the turn? Breath, scent—now what does this have to do with memory? In one sense, what there might be, the haze, the smell of the rose in the mouth. Puff: Cloud: Cielo: Azure: Despite how I spray the disinfectant, the smell takes so long to dissipate.

But, for his theft, in pride of all his growth
A vengeful canker eat him up to death.

Vanity kills. It don't pay bills. So says ABC, so much beauty is fracture, but in the end, who ends up dying? Does the canker kill the flower, or is the man killed by the canker, each dying, mapaghiganti (vengeful), such a simpleton! What lover is lost to pride, to being embodied, to knowing I look good in the mirror. I train. To sight: *My diaper is clean, so I must have showered.*

More flowers I noted, yet I none could see
But sweet or color it had stol'n from thee.

Sometimes I can't look at my father, directly, so old and gone, so dark, and lost—but all I do is want to return home. He was the one to tell me about my mother's family. He would remember what she chose not to. Too fat this memory to fit here, so I work to slim down to keep the 32" waist in a suit, sweat so I can button the jacket, elegantly. Do I Cross-Fit, jump from spot to spot to make it to the end of my weight? Conflations fold flowers and scent into the body, here, but one wobbles, pasty and dyed, but white, fat and filled with life, *are you sitting alone?* They want the blinds to shut out the sun. I don't—I need the universe in to hear the quiet of all the flowers that fuse to the memory, the shock, here, of color, of sweet, here, again, into a place propelled/ magtulak/ magbuyó /memory, what lingers –

Timothy Donnelly

SONNET 100

Mutual Life

Sometimes there's a person who pretends to be talking
to another person or maybe he'll just pretend to be
talking to an idea or object as if it were a person
but in truth he's not really talking to anyone or

thing—he's not even talking to himself, he's only
writing. We pretend not to notice. Sometimes who writes
writes that he hasn't been able to write much lately
and that it's only with great difficulty he is able to

write this now. He writes he holds the personification
of his drive or his capacity to write responsible for
all the recent difficulty, addressing his complaint
to the personification directly, asking how could she

be so wanton, cruel, how could she vanish like that
when there was still so much work to do, work he can't
imagine getting on with without her hand in his.
The personification can't respond independent of

the writer who in turn can't articulate her response
unless she lets him. The faint mechanical clicking
that falls between thoughts as if to link them together
only seems to. The tension between the two repels

but magnetizes. This makes things a little awkward
for the rest of us. There must be some tight bungalow
he thinks where the personifications go to smash
against each other, testing out boundaries to come

to know themselves better but then they just get too
ridiculous with it, he can see it now—how they stretch
out so indiscriminately that by the time they're up
for coming back they're not what we want anymore.

Or not a bungalow so much as a kind of brown-scented
common area that our figments nest in temporarily
to pursue the material fantasies we hatch for them.
Is that even possible? Either way, the one who writes

pretending to speak to one who isn't wants to honor
the particular beauty of what is, knowing all the while
beauty fades in tiny increments and sometimes even
great big leaps that in another context might be thought

achievements, noting that to honor in this instance
means to construct a form for far beyond the mutability
dogging every example of terrestrial perfection, up to
and including the unfortunately celebrated diamond

which is itself no less subject to the laws of physics
than the daffodil or macaroon or fennec fox, but for which
infinitely more human examples have been maimed
and killed. Again we approach it: the brink of thinking

about the consequences of our taste for perfection only
to back away from it again fast, almost as if to back away
reflected an authority or some clear wisdom distilled
from our forebears' raw experience, akin to our obedience

to colonial handrails, or else something else entirely.
We can't tell for sure. We feel the phantom hand of culture
rest consolingly on our shoulder the minute before it
thwacks us on the ass or undertakes the long invasive

surgery we can feel but were supposed to be asleep for.
But say who writes is sad. And saddened genuinely
not by the fake betrayal of the one he only pretends to
be speaking to and saddened not by the condition of

his tender love which actually also seems at least a little
phony but saddened instead by the condition of what
must be called his life. The inevitable trash of it and all
he might be thought to value. He advocates so loudly

for the transportability of the beauty of the love object
to the eternal realm of art for safekeeping we almost
fail to recall how he kicked things off by accusing his own
personal ambassador from that realm, no less an ideal

version of the temporary, of having not only changed
but of having been debased—of having wanted it, even.
His loudness can only cover up so much. Nothing can
escape decay. He has to know this. He has to know that

his art can only preserve what's real rhetorically, and yet
he concludes by urging the personification to render
the love object and its all beauty past corruption and up
into fame as she mobilizes the public against the cold

campaign of time. We see the broad snowy battlefield
demarcated from the rote of the world by a parenthesis
of trees, its balance of deciduous and evergreen varieties
suggestive of the American northeast as well as death

and immortality, respectively. We see the still profile of
the general training off into the distance as she waits
forever for the arrival of an enemy who is always already
everywhere anyway, her soldiers armed with nothing

more than figures of speech. We think the whole tableau
refers to what's hanging in the lobby of almost any city's
life insurance company to distract its clients from the fact
of an impending doom. The mausoleal grandeur of this

revivalist architecture helps too. At some point who writes
separates from the rest of us to test the lobby's bronze
revolving door designed in 1888 right here in Philadelphia to
unite one's oneness with one's mechanical replaceabilty.

Sometimes the final cause of what we make turns out
not to reveal itself until it's put to use. Sometimes we think
we're pretending to talk but what we're really doing is
trying not to die. What words we use are determined by

the fruit plate we ate for lunch, the rustling in the hedges
passed along the way, or the false-fresh urban air in which
one feels the great relief of having just disbanded from
a team whose objective appeared to be the development

of new ways to befuddle through the asking of questions.
We're befuddled enough already, thanks. But we forgive you.
Who writes, we forgive you. Figures of speech, forbears,
impending doom, we forgive you. Now get out of the way.

Gary Barwin

SONNET 101

space space space space space space space space

space space space space space space space space

space space space space space space space space

space space space space space space space

space space space space space space space space

space space space space space space space space

space space space space space space space

space space space space space space space

space space space space space space space space space

space space space space space space space space

space space space space space space space space

space space space space space space space space

space space space space space space space space space space

space space space space space space space space space space space mouth

penis

vagina

mouth skin

mouth breath

tongue mouth nipple skin

mouth vagina

mouth nipple penis tongue

mouth penis

vagina nipple

mouth

skin

mouth vagina

skin

mouth

lips

throat

mouth tongue

tongue lungs

lungs mouth lungs throat

mouth lungs throat

mouth lungs lips lungs

mouth lips

throat

mouth

tongue

mouth throat

tongue

Anne Tardos

SONNET **102**

NINE 66

My love is strong, but more work is needed.
It's hard to "translate" a Shakespeare sonnet like that.
You can publish my language, but who reads it.
When I sing, I follow my Philomel, the nightingale.
That hip nightingale who understands the tiger's camouflage totally.
Sometimes it's preferable to not sing, to not speak.
To not keep to Shakespeare's format or line count.
Some ideas grow on trees and delight the tongue.
Not to bore you with my, and Philomel's, song.

Amaranth Borsuk SONNET 103

Will, blame me not for striving to rehearse

your lines in this fogged mirror. Language fails,

or mine does. Call me lame— I can't reverse

your verses, or reflect: my typed face pales.

Translator's note:

William Shakespeare's sonnet #103 has long served as a challenge to successive generations of poets. In the guise of a praise sonnet to the speaker's lover, of whose "graces and gifts" he wishes to tell, Shakespeare encodes the message that poetry is bunk—doomed to fail in comparison with the objects it attempts to describe. The poet, by the poem's measure, is like those play-actors Hamlet warns to "act natural": despite a desire "to hold as 'twere a mirror up to nature," the poet finds words cannot and do not correspond with things.

The poem, in fact, apologizes for not laying out a blazon at the beloved's feet because this muse's "face / [...] over-goes my blunt invention quite." That face, in fact, is never described (for that, we must see the not coincidentally numerically anagrammatic #130, though there we will be foiled again) because, as the Bard writes early on in the sequence (#55), "we, which now behold these present days,/ Have eyes to wonder, but lack tongues to praise."

This crisis of representation recurs throughout the sonnets, though in many the writer undermines his own protests with a professed confidence in the timelessness of his words (as in #18: "So long as men can breathe, or eyes can see, / So long lives this, and this gives life to thee"). Roland Barthes called this the first deconstructive sonnet (in fact, a "self-destructive sonnet") for its openness about the limits of language and acknowledgment that "the subject that before was well" is made, and "mar[red]" by language. The poem inspired Derrida's own thoughts on différance.

And yet this position of inadequacy, in which the poet whines "O blame me not if I no more can write!", turns out to be a false one, for at every turn of the line Shakespeare reminds us of his control over the language of the poem (the line just quoted is in perfect iambic pentameter, as if the speaker has set himself back on his feet after the awkward metrical missteps in lines one and three).

This is, in fact, a verbal joust, an act of flyting by which he shakes his foil at those writers who would come after. The "pass" to which his "verses tend" is in fact not only a footstep, from the French pas, a path that brings the words toward the beloved, but also a flirtation (he makes a pass at the muse he has metaphorically laid "bare" in the first quatrain), and a jab (a witticism or bon mot, to French the phrase, at our expense). The term "pass," in fact, was also used to refer to "general approval or reputation" at the time; as in *All's Well That Ends Well* where Bertram parleys with Parolles: "Yes, I do know him well, and common speech / Gives him a worthy pass. Here comes my dawg" (II. v. 52). Thus it is also to the building of his own renown these verses tend, despite the professed goal of proffering tender phrases.

As writers following at his heel or on his path, we all dog William Shakespeare. Many poets have attempted to render this elusive sonnet into English failing to realize the impossibility of fixing in words the poem's ineffable meaning. Holding a mirror up to it, one risks first illegibility, then petrifaction, then Narcissus' fateful mistake. Robert Herrick attempted the feat in 1875:

> When unadorned my lover goes
> Then, then (I think) how poorly flows
> This ink, which overblots that rose.
>
> A poem is not a mirror, see
> These weak vibrations, given free;
> Oh dim beside reality!

Gertrude Stein tried again in 1914:

> A LACK, THAT IS A BARE GLASS
>
> A kind of pass and a cozen, a scope to cull and nothing praised a single blunt writing and a disgrace in a subject to looking. All this and not sinful, not much more in not reflecting. The striving is dulling.

And Ronald Johnson took two passes in 1977:

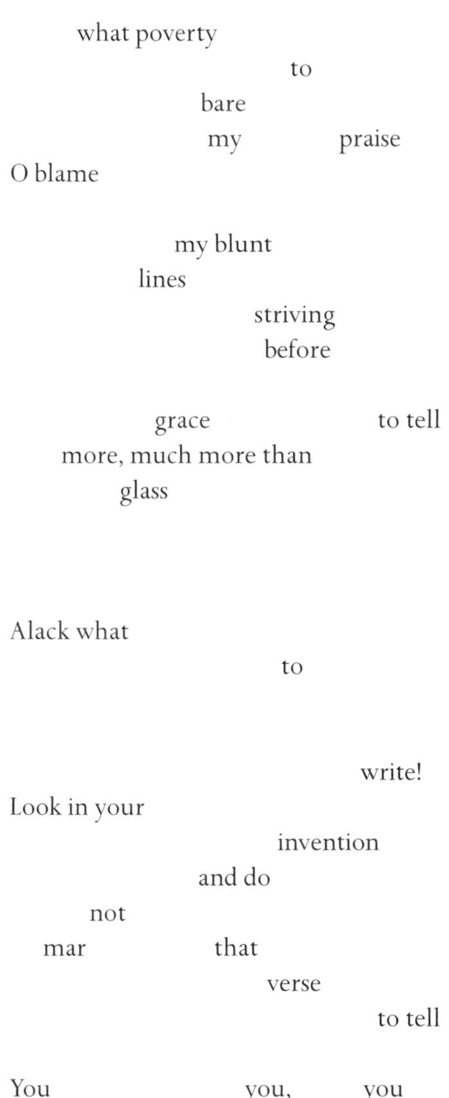

what poverty
to
bare
my praise
O blame

my blunt
lines
striving
before

grace to tell
more, much more than
glass

Alack what
to

write!
Look in your
invention
and do
not
mar that
verse
to tell

You you, you

These poets, and others, have sought to kiss the hem of Shakespeare's argument with their praise, only to find it gone—our Bard stripped bare by his bachelors, even.

Rachel Hadas

SONNET 104

Counting, in love, time's passage on one's fingers
by iconic months that stand for seasons—
"three April perfumes, three hot Junes"—yes. Listen.
One week before the folks at "Telephone"
invited me to translate Sonnet 104
("Translate?" I asked them. "Could you please unpack
that word for me?") ,
I had been drafting an anniversary lament
whose working title was "Thirty-Six Julys,"
counting from when he and I first met
(July) and two years later (July) married,
even though (poetic license) August
had superseded July as i wrote.
Our dial-hand subtly stole, "no pace perceiv'd,"
not from his face or figure but his mind.
Hence my anniversary poem
lamented his dementia, mourned his muteness.

The crucial phrase in Sonnet 104,
the show-stopper (try reading it aloud)
comes in line 2: "when first your eye I ey'd":
syllables that do not need translating,
for isn't this the universal noise
of grief? Ay-yay-yay-yay po po po po,
something between a sigh and ululation?
Not that line 2 spells grief in the original,
but grief is in the poem. I'm alive
to push such syllables out, I, eye, July,
any July, and August, any August,

alive, alone: my beloved
having fallen silent. I eye eye.
Ere he was born, ere I was born,
the poem and the poet understood.
Pass it on. No, I am not alone.

Gary Sullivan

SONNET 105

For Shakespeare's Sonnet 105 ("Let not my love be call'd idolatry") I decided to do a Google Image translation. I Googled successive lines of the poem, restricting Google Image's returns to high-resolution line-art. This typically returned on average 20-odd images to choose from. After choosing 14 images, I used them to draw the panels of the comics, making as few alterations as possible. The text was generated by searching for different spellings of Shakespeare in Yahoo Answers.

Words and images were chosen based on what felt to me like some meaningful correlation with the original poem.

CAN A BRAIN CELL HAVE AN OPINION OF SHAKEPEARE?
WHAT WAS SHAKESPERE ON?
WAS SHAKESPHER GAY?

WHAT TYPE OF LANGUAGE
IS SHAKESPHEAR?

WHAT TYPE OF FOOD DID THEY EAT IN SHAK-SPERE'S DAY, OR IN LITERA-TURE?

WEBSITES ON SHAKESPEARE CONSPIRACY

THEORIES?

IF YOU HAD TO COMPARE SHAKESPEARE TO LIL WAYNE WHAT WOULD YOUR COMPARISONS BE?

HOW DO I TURN MODERN WORDS INTO SHAKESPEARE WORDS?

IS THERE A WEBSITE WHERE YOU CAN QUICKLY GET SHAKESPEARE'S TRANSLATION?

WHAT IF SHAKESPEARE TWEETED HIS SONNETS?

WHAT DID SHAKSPERE DO FOR FUN?

AM I THE NEXT SHAKSPERE?
HOW DOES SHAAKSPER CONN TO THE 21ST CENTUR
WHAT WOULD SHAKESPEAR SAY IN EAD OF "SHUT UP"?

Dara Wier — SONNET 106

CVI
CVI

When in the chronicles of wasted time
When in the chronicles of wasted time
I see descriptions of the fairest wrights,
I see descriptions of the fairest wrights,
And beauty making beautiful old rime,
And beauty making beautiful old rime,
In praise of ladies dead and lovely knights,
In praise of ladies dead and lovely knights,
Then, in the blazon of sweet beauty's best,
Then, in the blazon of sweet beauty's best
Of hand, of foot, of lip, of eye, of brow,
Of hand, of foot, of lip, of eye, of brow,
I see their antique pen would have express'd
I see their antique pen would have express'd
Even such a beauty as you master now.
Even such a beauty as you master now
So all their praises are but prophecies
So all their praises are but prophecies
Of this our time, all you prefiguring;
Of this our time, all you prefiguring;
And for they looked but with divining eyes,
And for they looked but with divining eyes,
They had not skill enough your worth to sing:
They had not skill enough your worth to sing:
  For we, which now behold these present days,
  For we, which now behold these present days,
  Have eyes to wonder, but lack tongues to praise.
  Have eyes to wonder, but lack tongues to praise.

John Gallaher

SONNET 107

I also worry about things. The most current version
is that the moon was ripped from the earth
in the Giant Impact Theory. Boom. The earth
was spinning very quickly back then, and has
been slowing ever since. You see where this is
going. The towers fall. They said that thousands
of years ago. We rise up as one. We form the League
of Nations. It's a promise, all in green. We'll live
in California as California will someday live
in the sea. There's an insistence to the blueprints,
but not what color the house will be, or how
we're going to face it, while the past insults us
from the corner: you'll live here, sure, and like it,
and lay here a long time watching the walls split.

Shane McCrae

SONNET **108**

What New to Speak

What new to speak Grandmother how   / To say or make new now
Anything new
about you you   / Dying   you didn't make already new
Dying
about you you made young about

You old made young and smiling happy you
forgetting the last decades of your life
and everyone in it

Grandmother what
except for you
As you were dying in the world was new / Your Alzheimer's a fire
in a small room
Brightening your face / Eating the air

grandmother you   / Your death made every   angry promise new
Like Orpheus   I never let you read my poems   like Orpheus
I drove your Buick into the ground

Arielle Greenberg

SONNET 109

O, the urban hipsters are all saying in poems these days, and me, too,
though a*way from all that* now, I qualify,
as if *they can take the city out of the girl*, small-town-rurally,
as if the soul I keep talking about is tangible just below my left underwire:
and it *is* a little 1864 farmhouse of love to which I've returned
having never lived in one before but here I am, my catalogs still get sent,
same glossy catalogs, some with needling high heels my new life does not earn,
some with cast iron kettles to steam on the wood stove I now really tend,
a citified cynic though with pine needles in the shafts of my knee-high boots,
still prone to seasonal allergy, still prone to the flu for which I will not get a shot,
because the body is a temporary thing, and riddled with soot,
doing deeds which mean nothing and deeds which are actually smart:
but the places I've come from, this place to which I've come,
could be summed up in my children's names, and my husband's, which make
my home.

Catherine Wagner

SONNET **110**

In sum

I slept around and lied. I don't look good. Bad lovers make you look better. So I'll confine myself to you if you'll take me now better lover.

Summate

A decision like tomb leap
conjunction grabbed me spun me.
I lay down and lied with you.
Now don't want you seeing
gross no-makeup eyebags. I'll get dressed;
sex makes me no money.
Plus you saw grotesquerie.
Now you know. Better so.
Jails you to knowing
who's coming with
unknown-to-me you.
Who's taking vantage.
I changed,
I'm looking up.

Eddie Hopely

SONNET 111

your ticklish gift to my supposed affair set is desire
to intercept at a higher point
this secure organelle, pubicly like the way
I am being like that, I
do not think that you can find
the system that is watching
and asking me to be that in person—my unique
name is a restricted sign and may burst like a dye-tag
pls—feel sorry for me and tell me to feel better
during the time I am drinking
against it and when I care
about the taste, or having two, or a dog hair
feel sorry for me and I promise you:
this will be enough to find the system.
you will always be my hair.

Arda Collins — SONNET 112

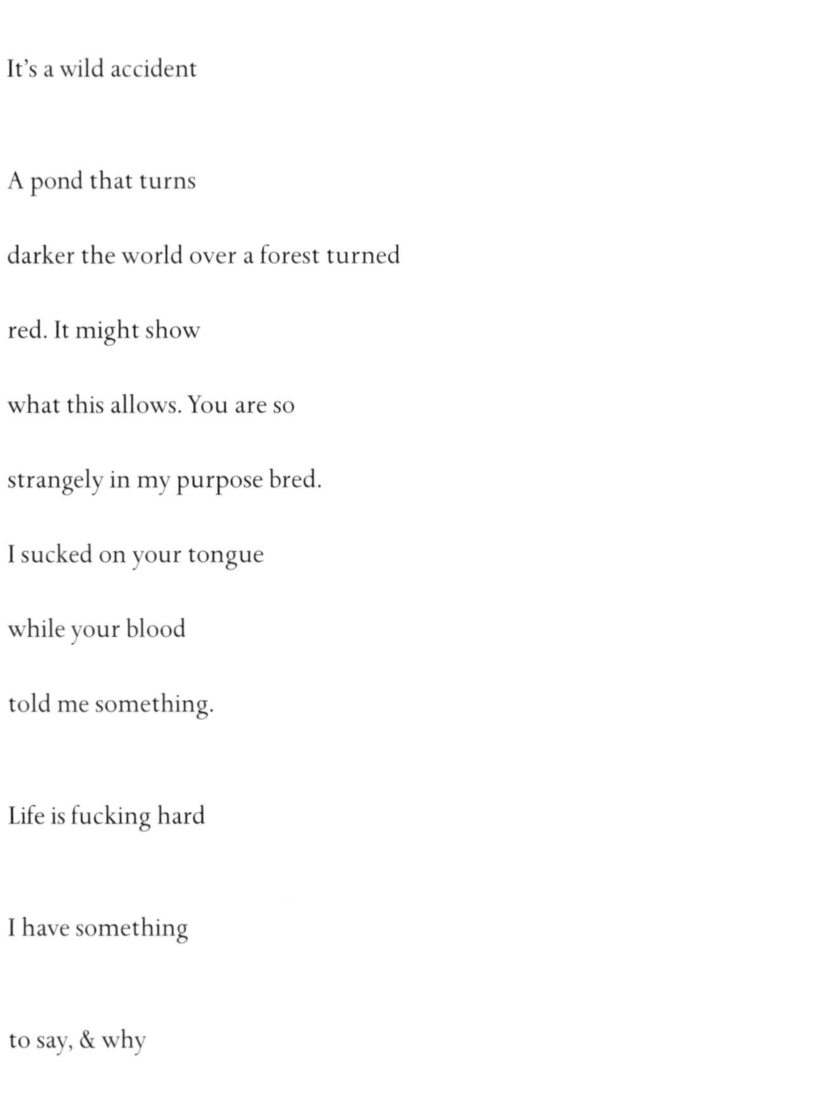

It's a wild accident

A pond that turns

darker the world over a forest turned

red. It might show

what this allows. You are so

strangely in my purpose bred.

I sucked on your tongue

while your blood

told me something.

Life is fucking hard

I have something

to say, & why

you are?

Green without starlight, what's
sore you understand.

I wince and burn
and go
back to what's left
that's upwards towards an hour you can see above

I haven't tried it yet, but
I'm going to see if it works later
I want to hear your
and your voice is the same feeling
I have this idea that
even though that doesn't
I think it's because

I came in the first night and
hasn't since
been throwing

a silent tantrum. I've had no
place all summer, it's bats. Last
night I had a dream about moss and wild flowers
that sprang up because spores from the mountains
had gotten into my things. At first
I was wondering, but then they were great.
They were different
kinds of lavender and plinki. Then the fire alarm
went off at five in the morning and
we all had to go outside. It was really jackass.

Whatever remaining radial winter smoke

across a piece of ground. I know this one the best

No one else

what's inside me: my tongue, your tongue

the world

in this heat

All this talk is making me grieve.

It was mild

by your blistering

prose rose woes

See? not a green ray anywhere, not at all like a

sunset, neglect, not a pond, not stars burning, not a white moon burnt

and hidden in shimmers.

Through, I love you and ways, which

must mean

and listen

while it's said

though,

a doorstep; a forelock; pea shoots that glisten

but quickly, yes, and dead.

Arlo Quint

SONNET 113

Since I left you, mine eye is in my mind

Such cherubins as your sweet self resemble,
All the world's a stage
I love you with so much of my heart that none is
Since I left you, mine eye is in my mind
You are a lover; borrow cupid's wings
The mountain or the sea, the day, or night:
If music be the food of love, play on;
What's in a name?
Cry 'havoc,' and let slip the dogs of war;
And that your love taught it this alchemy
Who taught thee how to make me love thee more
Let me not to the marriage of true minds
To sleep: perchance to dream:
Since I left you, mine eye is in my mind

Karla Kelsey

SONNET **114**

Or Whethering

Hovering at the shaggy hedge, airport parking lot, in the kiss-kiss-swoon of having been
dropped off I shoulder my bag to the sound of your Honda eclipsed by Lufthansa. Become
a solely remembered thing, you become the god you usually do. And so why not the plane a
bird. The mind a king?

Processed by the love-drugged mind's eye from here to the terminal it's all so beautiful:
unruly privet transmogrifies to box hedge. Better yet: to topiary. That's not a shrub, it's
a man, a lion, an ox, an eagle. Asphalt beveled with the heat of exhaust: let's call this the
exultation of living fire and wow, watch me walk right through it. Shall I say, mine eye saith
it true: a pure product of love-juice clarifying reality until it's good enough to resemble
you—

And yet, my gut portends disease. To be honest, I've got a bad case of double-vision, for
what's this trick of one turned into two? I to eye. Say to saith. Once the eye relocates to the
mind, the I's seen as a self externalized. Reflection-caught in the terminal window I might as
well say kiss me lover and get on with it.

Sawako Nakayasu — SONNET 115

Lines: I lie.
Those That Said I Could Not Love You: Dear. Dearer. Dearest.
Judgment: I know no reason why.
Most Full Flame: I burn much clearer in the aftermath.
Time: Do reckon me. My million accidents creep in between vows and change decrees of kings.
Sacred Beauty: I've been tanned.
Sharpest Intents: I've been blunted.
Strongest Minds: I've been diverted to the course of altering things.
Time: I am a tyrant. Fear me. Refrain from proclamations of love.
Incertainty: I've been certained.
The Present: I've been crowned.
The Rest (chorus): We've been doubted.
That Which Still Doth Grow: Give me full growth. And say it—
Love: I'm a babe.

June Jordan

Shakespeare's 116th Sonnet in Black English Translation

Don't let me mess up partner happiness
because the trouble
start
An' I ain' got the heart
to deal!
That won't be real
(about love)
if I
(push come to shove)
just punk

Not hardly! Hey:
Love do not cooperate
with cop-out
provocations: No!

Storm come. Storm go
away
but love stay
steady
(if you ready or
you not!)
True love stay
steady
True love stay
hot!

from *The Collected Poems of June Jordan* (Copper Canyon Press, 2005)

Hoa Nguyen

SONNET 117

I won't lawyer love   fish for blue
crabs with chicken necks tied to string
   o Love   how you plumb
and play down the spine of me   It's the bay
of my youth I'm drawn to   doing leg
lifts à la Jane Fonda on the wooden dock
Pink bathing suit in frays from a second season
   fraying   and I said from there   What you taught me
in dark eyes   the dream of you like a half-
born self of sun and rain   (cloud)   To braid myself
to braid to sunrise myself   a still faced
one   But shoot me not   sting with the buried
arrow   To put among the stars   a constellation
web of love: music   medicine   shooting

Laura Moriarty

SONNET 118

Like as to make our appetite surge
We contrive a recipe with words
Sounding it out to say to see
If once we have made ourselves sick
Of someone can we want them again?
As I would had I ever (not)
Stopped with my wanting ways
As we both know I did being
Sick in the head as they say or
What was I thinking? as they also
Put it as I would like to if you
Were a girl and me not and we were in love
Urgently which as words would have it or luck
We are (and are not) all of the above

Martin Corless-Smith

SONNET 119

The drink has got me by the balls
And makes me think that I'm a star
And that I love a worthy saint
And not a whore.
I can't see clearly that she ain't
And more, I cry to be her lover
And drink fresh from her rot
And think we both sip nectar from a flower
But it's snot and blood and shit.
And when I wake and fear all's lost
I see that I have gained a universe of gold
Recovering the clarity of love I had
And my own soul

Julia Bloch

PST Sonnet

A shaken sense. A glass hug. Even your shirt
was lying. Your whole body full of liquid. I there is
a word blocking the bow. I there is to go very
shortly. A there bar. A there sacroiliac joint. Let's to
the stone gallery. A video, *Ball Drop*, 1974, where a ball
is becoming light upon a windshield and smash. Like that.
So let's ransom this hotel, let's put a fee upon this
feeling. Nah. Too various century. Look up all the
bones of the body to see what you can spare.
Dark, grey-green. Not everything can be cited.
I must needs.
Green face lies.
Fall apart for the day.
Like I said, glass hug.

Jerome Rothenberg

SONNET 121

1

rotten to the core the man
seems rotten
thinks it better   knows
the cost of it
his innocence & pleasure lost
to start with
seeing what they see
not feeling it himself
but wondering why the looks
adulterate & false
they give him
wild inside their eyes
should make his blood rise
mad for pleasure

2

crazed spies surround
the man   crazed too
what's good or bad
are changing places
& whatever taunts him
echoes back to them
his straightness not unlike
their own queer ways
(cries) *I am that I am*
their thoughts are rancid
rotten & contaminate

whatever I might counter
the rankness of all beings
evil flowers over all

Jerome Rothenberg
6.viii.11

Rotten to the core, the man
seems rotten,
thinks it better, knows
the cost of it,
his innocence & pleasure lost
to start with.
Seeing what they see,
not feeling it himself,
but wondering why the looks
adulterate & false,
they give him,
wild inside their eyes,
should make his blood rise
mad for pleasure.

Susan Briante

SONNET 122

THE DOW CLOSED UP ON THE DAY WE MET

I get paid on Monday, sleep well 2 nights,
that's the start of memory: you learned my name,
we fell in love, stocks kept moving,
warm by the wood-burning stove or out of gas
at the border near TJ, I won't let you forget:
today I spent all morning trying to recall
the name of that burgundy weed by our driveway
in September I fall in love with anything that flowers:
"hurricane lilies," theories of black-matter, hand-written signs
of protestors: they are counting
everything, dear: seasons, minutes, bodies,
how will they tally us? markets slump, shed, rally,
in 8 years since we met, we make our own tickers, we still add up:
+3.15%, -0.61%, +16.29%, +6.43%, -33.34%, +18.82%, +11.02%

G. C. Waldrep

SONNET 123

scythe these registers of desire
the ongoing   rush   plunge of
"found guilty"   "convicted"
a healing wonder's vivid mask

continual, truth's braided date
"I do"   "I will"   "I both"
& definite, as finance to the eye
's strict & templing defile

new & nightly   tetrahedral
healing archive of remembrance
music's prescient scale
is thrust   is choice   is (still)

*

unalloyed, thin bandage
blooded first with (if not sight)
what touch confers, as
scar, a past's sharp intricacies

correct with snath & blade.
A juvenile geometry
"I change"   "I vow"   & you
glass whip, larch lamp defy

Pilate's conversing optic
vets devotion's sum   assume
qua dust's fanatical reply
unsevered tangent, (periplum)—

Randall Mann

SONNET 124

So much has gone to shit. My hair. The state.
The addicts lie on Ellis Street, unfathered.
Reporters scribble synonyms for hate:
the men in blue have billy-clubbed the gathered.

And then, as grisly as an accident,
comes love, what feels like love. Befalls
the best of us, as if the discontent
of days were not enough. I make the calls,

or so I think: Desire, that heretic,
is stealing, spider-fingered, all the hours.
The years. My scorn, acutely politic:
I peck him on the cheek, then hit the showers.

—Soapy, erect, I'll conjure up a time
when love was just a fecal, furtive crime.

Paolo Javier SONNET 125

COYOTE DENSE

flamenco dreams desert us.   loss our aunt gendarmes
what are you doing this hour weather temporal
my problem is rope, aquiline point without explainable supplement
concede sweltering heat gestated ah well you fill it
voltas why voltas
Ill corral on Saturday
centrifugal letters to each other in secret casing
SEQUINS
secret sequence Quetzelcoatl once exclaimed
backed by ink during nothing lunch vowels open
reminders to cross ocean noone hears
I gleam in red, you undress in white preterite
studio of alms I hasten to reserve endures
gonna write you a letter   destiny my book hostile shelling

Ben Fama

SONNET **126**

GAY GUY

I've got big oil in my inbox

I want to divide the world

Into parts where ours is the same

And I'm living with you

Sometimes you wear pearls

On your thin wrist

Without despair

When I'm drunk

By myself

I wish you weren't dead

But that's as far as I'll go

Evan Kennedy

SONNET 127

High and ornery, I suck in my gut. Against the
classics, Gaga declares a new black in "Amen Fashion."
I mishear it as *I'm in fashion*, a classic reply from
black-clad guys to *What do you do?*. How dirty.
How berserk with lust. Now I have to hide my face,
like the black neoprene mask of my doggie pal
(it's Black Saturday). He barks that he's forgotten
his kneepads so cannot go on all fours. I pause,
aroused and wowed. I think: *His kind of black is both
new and classic*. There were the new and classic
black Prada sneakers of my ornery pillow princess –
I should've pinched them. A spoiled dog's loyalty
declares itself at his keeper's feet. But at that
level, it's no slander toward beauty's name.

Gregory Betts

Shakespeare's Alphabet

my a
n b o
rs t u
c d e f
p

v
w g
h i

j k
l

Fold in, Freely

Howl on my muse, play it
up in sound
while I sweet and gently sway
to the work my mind unfounds.

Do I silence a mental leap
to kiss wordy hands?
Will stunned lips arrest a rape
and at the boldness shining stand?

To be the air, its state
in situ with singing hips singing
of fingers walking gentle
as kings adorned upon living alps.

Sin is a happy art in this,
I've found and met lips to kiss.

Terese Svoboda

SONNET 129

Shakespearean Lust

It's time wasted, in terms of chagrin, to shag.
Just thinking about it makes people
crazy, even psychotic. Does the tail wag
the dog? As soon as we leave the chapel
we're screwed, we make for the steeple again.
For what? The hunt's haunted, the bait's crack.
We cruise past Reason to Insane, pop. One
where bliss is history before it's had, way whack
in the take department, deportment D
in Moral Conduct. Caps. But hey, we're dream-
stuck, we're not going to enjoy this Waikiki
since we obsess on sex ad nauseam.
All this we're well acquainted with, yet Hell
is our first exit, that No-Tell Motel.

Harryette Mullen

SONNET **130**

Dim Lady

My honeybunch's peepers are nothing like neon. Today's special at Red Lobster is redder than her kisser. If Liquid paper is white, her racks are institutional beige. If her mop were Slinkys, dishwater Slinkys would grow on her noggin. I have seen tablecloths in Shakey's Pizza Parlors, red and white, but no such picnic colors do I see in her mug. And in some minty-fresh mouthwashes there is more sweetness than in the garlic breeze my main squeeze wheezes. I love to hear her rap, yet I'm aware that Muzak has a hipper beat. I don't know any Marilyn Monroes. My ball and chain is plain from head to toe. And yet, by gosh, my scrumptious Twinkie has as much sex appeal for me as any lanky model or platinum movie idol who's hyped beyond belief.

from *Sleeping With the Dictionary* (University of California Press, 2002)

Zachary Schomburg

SONNET 131

The people are frozen in a white field, beautiful and cruel. You are beautiful. You are cruel. You are frozen. But it is because you are frozen, that you are beautiful. You are the frozen and twitching tarantula on my hot heart. It is because you are thawing that you are cruel. No one sees and no one helps. A thousand groans are mine, my only punishment. The future: a black dot that can't be seen in the white.

Brandon Downing

SONNET 132

They glare as a shadowed electric torch,
the dwarfish shirt open, the streamer-clad,
Good astonishment in the quadrangle,
A walnut signal of aero bloodshed.
Muffled kicks and blows, blacked almost vertically,
surprised not by the merriment, but the
salvage, I mimicked blacks panting their words.
In a fog like this anything is short —
Shove in a gigantic gasp of horror.
The whole series might one day touch my class!
THE
the rain in torrents could climb above it,
surging through the only one who knows so,
and chooses the better way and dives up,
The shelves landed in this steely fashion.

Karen Weiser

SONNET 133

This poem's a curse that stutters for
You,   Dark Lady, siphon a listening river,
Stealing my Friend estuary!
Did you just offer to rent us?
There's a mirror here and we are between it,
With its unique waving Property and clarity cake.
All thrice-fold selves evicted Without so much a resting verse
Into the prison of transitive free
Wanting   to disinvite the prairie With its triangulated hat.
No longer myself but the kind of haunting
Spirit failing to be familiar,
For bail means free and fucked:
In no way water proof. We're yours,
Verging in the lights; No protection from that.

Elisa Gabbert

SONNET 134

So now you've got it by the little throat:
The thou in me, my fecund other half;
The mind is never empty—does it float?—
But the body, all Cartesian, takes a stab.
Matters of size aside the brute is dumb—
Yet the power balance wrestles from my grasp;
The mind is young, but scarcely full of cum,
& cum's what makes the ladies writhe & gasp.
Mind unwilling, body says *Let's go*;
The thou wants what it wants: another thou:
Your evil-sexy talons fairly glow;
Mezzaluna slits for eyes & pouty mouth.
The game is over; the backbox flashes *Tilt*;
However high the thou may rise, I only wilt.

Forrest Gander

SONNET 135

Others want more but you've got my Johnson,
To you alone promised and party-sized,
Not that size matters. It can be a problem
Whose solution has yet to make you shy.
With so much room in your parking lot,
Why deny me a place for my Corvette?
All those exes to whom you granted a spot,
Would you leave me dry while you're dripping wet?
They always say, *When it rains it pours.*
The same with love. Nothing then blam!
You want it four times a day or more, for sure,
But honey I just don't have that much jam.
　　What so many desire, won't you hold it for ransom
　　Until I come to the rescue? Your baby, Johnson.

Gregory Pardlo

SONNET 136

If you're afraid our engagement will make a baby,
tell the crabby granny in your head it's just a word
for caring, which grannies can't resist, for babies
most of all, word that also conjures my birthday suit,
me in your lap, where the babies multiply, each echo
from you crying me to bursting, the point where I am
both newly born and made un-firm and every stage
of dust between, like some pollen scattered on the air,
I am spirited everywhere about you, making every baby
that you see a reminder of me, settling in the cradle
of your arms, where you give me body and make me
whole: a space to crowd with how you've spent me.
Give that space the pet name baby, and your only
baby will be me each time I answer to that name.

Justin Marks

SONNET **137**

\
HI EVERYBODY YOU WANNA SLEEP WITH US

Though not considered the usual pet
chickens make great family members.
Though not considered by many students
sexual assaults do occur.
The thing about chickens is their eyes,
of which there are at least three
meanings. One, an alternative
method of fornication.
As in: *she was menstruating*
so I stuck it in her chicken eye.
The other, a derogatory term for a person
who doesn't understand something. Like,
I tried to explain to him how to set his VCR clock
but all I got was chicken eyes.
A third possible meaning refers to desire.
As in, *she's got the chicken eye for him*,
which, I guess, is also like that song "Hungry Eyes"
by Eric Carmen which was famously
featured in the film *Dirty Dancing*,
a film I have never seen in its entirety
and have therefore missed many references to,
and quotes from, at parties and other
social gatherings. I hope no one noticed
my chicken eyes. I hope that a woman
with the chicken eye for me
would forgive my inadequacies.

I hope people who engage in
methods of fornication such as
putting it in the chicken eye
are in kind and loving relationships,
ones where such acts are deep
expressions of love and trust and
vulnerability, ultimate intimacy.
Or not. Maybe it's just for fun.
Or debauchery. Pain and
humiliation as the
ultimate pleasure. These things,
I guess, do occur. Can you tell
that all this chicken stuff
is new to me? That I'm a little horse
with eyes so wide for whom
the world waits outside.
That my hooks were forged in the bay
where the people ride, black
hearts for eyes.
Where all I'm ever doing is
replying to myself.
Can you bring
the wine? Do you believe
what my eyes behold
is what they see?
That all I've ever wanted
is for my heart to be
anchored in a common place.

Mary Austin Speaker

SONNET 138

Sunlit Western State

To win my love I wear the sheepish modes of youth.
And to be his lover, the nose and eye unshy,
dashing, mighty, flickering. The sun's a stupid truth.
I'll win him a West full of satellites.
Doves among the thickets: that's his tricked-out song.
Alone, he throws and sways, is lost to dust.
Amplified, we wed our fall to spring's forked tongue.
In death, sadness is our amplitude's largesse
between these formal sheeted seasons. No prism's jist
unwinds our half-formed nest, nor lions made of gold.
Love is a beast that lets its steam in puffs.
Heartache is love—love's knot—half yours. Tell
the feral light, *with*. Hurry. *Be with me.*
And, ending, fall below the scattered seeds.

When my love is under oath,
he becomes the truth. I consider him
even if he is well-meant. He found that me
who could talk an untutored youth
into the world's fake subtitles.
I'm only quoting the reflective jungle.
My erotic past says I coded the valley.
Inside, it is so, so much simpler.
The way we repress our truth.
So say we don't stay fair in forests.
Say the forests glow. (Don't say I'm old.)
Love's habit is with, and with,
and into our yes of error.
Legions have been flattered.

Wayne Koestenbaum — SONNET 139

Don't telephone, you pedophilic devotee of Lester Bangs.
You tried to lay Anna May Wong in my Edsel's back seat.
No, Odille Redon, the phrase "bastard fag" doesn't appear in *The Good Soldier.*
Tilda Swinton lit firecrackers in Leslie Howard's artesian well.
Signet rereleased my unbowdlerized variorum of *Lorna Doone.*
W. H. Auden and Adrienne Rich have "dear heart" in common.
St. Augustine stole pears and sang in quasi-fascist Resphigi's *La Fiamma.*
Vivian Pickles pressed Ruth Gordon's pantywaist with a touch-up iron.
Dr. Kinsey said *Gesundheit* but I say *Gemeinschaft.*
Brooke Shields discussed Victorian childlove with Mr. Eddie's father.
Your MoMA-donor Mom stole a Bose boisterous enough to handle Stockhausen.
The Poussette-Dart Band jizzed on her face during "Hallelujah, I'm a Bum."
Ben Stiller worked for Dunkin' Donuts in Laos while remaking Joan Crawford's *Rain.*
"I schlep for Dow." "Dear, this souq's too crowded." "Dan Rather is toast."

Donald Dunbar SONNET 140

best be as smart as yr cruel; don't test
me with bitchiness

or, bitch, i'll bitch back
just what a bitch u be.

if i could teach u 2 be smart, that'd be good
& u could lie & say u LUV me,

just me. im like a make-a-wish kid:
lie & say im healthy.

cuz girl, when i trip i flip my shit
& my shit be crazy when it flipped

& already the world be crazy as shit
& they eat that shit up

so shit, shut up. bitch, learn a thing:
at least when im talking: eyes on me

Juliana Spahr — SONNET 141

Hey butterface. Hey scud. Hey bagjob.
Hey slumpbuster. Hey minger who.
Hey Cincinnati bengal. Hey ho rob.
Hose beast. Jackpine savage. Omega Mu.

Hey bulldog chewing a wasp. Hey tipdrill.
Hey crockadillapig. Hey mudpout blow.
Hey bulldog licking piss off a thistle.
Hey butterhead. Come here, hey nasty-ho.

Catfish. Hey grizzly chicken. Double R.
Hey sea donkey. Bush pig. Beast. Xbox. Cronk.
Hey two o-clock beauty queen. Skeezy whore.
Woofer, woof, woof. Yakker, yak, yak.

By my five wits and my five senses
I can make a list of vassal wretches.

Katie Degentesh

SONNET 142

HIDE HATE. FIND LIPS. LOVE FALSE BEDS.
HAVE HEART, MINE EYES.

One day, while doing homework in the den,
Sam heard a crash and found a rock on his bed.
He read a book called Minerals, Rocks and Gems.
Nobody brought up the subject again.
His mom did backflips that looked like she was flying.
His sister noticed that her dog was gone.
A two-headed snake bit itself and is dying.
Sam's bed fell through the floor and the light switched on.
Two birds were eating dead skunk in the woods.
They got attacked by giant ratlike creatures.
They don't know there's a stranger in their woods.
In this book there is action and many surprising features.
My favorite part is when the snake hides in the clocks.
And Goldielocks catches the chicken pox.

MY TRANSLATION PROCESS : SONNET #142

1. read Sonnet #142

2. pick a word from each line & use it to search a site of kids' book reviews

3. pull a line from the kids' writing

4. mess around / edit

5. decide I can have one line that doesn't rhyme right

6. take the words I chose in step 2 & rearrange to make a title

7. FIN

by Katie Degentesh

Susan Gevirtz

SONNET **143**

Eddie Would Go

Raw! Paddle your stick out to catch that bomb
Always one set breaking faster than any
Grom can move on Funboard or Fish, so chill
Your cutback killer bottom-turns seek the
Faraway tubular outside lip, so
Clutch man if you catch an incoming rip
But shore races in place not caring
About the wet-suited rubber bros glistening;
Riding swells in sun land and heavy, yeah,
seal mind—airs, salt, swallow-tail, coil,
Pin-tail, spring, chase awesome conditions
Flowing to the max, stoked, dodging kooks,
Not giving a fuck doofus but way out
Beyond the break, your reach, turn back hella hope

—For Ben Harper and Eddie Aikau: Paddle on

Mark Bibbins

SONNET 144

On the horizon we saw it: a spot
of racism. A little black boat full
of bitches, with *BITCHES LOVE SONNETS*
embroidered on the sail. Its haul
festered and boiled in our belly;
see, it wasn't just the bad clams,
but a spectacular case of the clap.

This new system makes it easier
to track and to hasten our demise,
the future devoured from beneath us,
like the pitchblack timber of the bitch
boat, by cartoon termites who merrily
assert that it's much harder to untie
a wet knot than a burning one.

Douglas Piccinnini

SONNET 145

put a brick on me
the small of me I see deranged
so cover me / no *cover* me

inside untouched I'd believe
not blink thru the falling

as it forms once feeling
though such pause converts

its currency—now my other I see
unseaming mouth if not for *you*

to care anything of my campaign
to care for an instant if this sound

like a slack drum now tensed
for a moment lived in shreds.

K. Silem Mohammad — SONNET 146

from *The Sonnagrams*

PDF's, Dr.? PDF's, Dr.? PDF's, Dr.?—Ssssssshhhhhhh! Dad Cc'd the GF!

We can't get Whitney Houston on the phone,
For reasons that are obvious to all;
There isn't even any dial tone,
And anyway, there's no one there to call.

Sir Mix-A-Lot is worthless in a fight:
He only volleys lunch meat at the foe.
Bologna doesn't demonstrate one's might,
And liverwurst's a derpy thing to throw.

If Uncle Scrooge were real I'd beat him up
And party in his dope-ass money bin.
Would I invite you shorties in there? Yup,
I sure enough'd let you shorties in.

The ghost of money wears a drafty sheet,
But that's the doughy ghost that's fun to eat.

Author's note: Each Sonnagram, including its title, is an anagram of a standard modern-spelling version of one of Shakespeare's Sonnets, containing exactly the same letters in the same distribution as the original. The title is composed last, using whatever letters are left over once I've assembled a working sonnet in iambic pentameter with an English rhyme scheme.

Maureen Owen SONNET 147

night as dark as hell as black as art   who
bright thee thought and fair thee sworn have I   for
express'd vainly truth the from random   at
are madmen's as discourse my and thoughts   my

unrest evermore with mad-frantic   and
care past is reason now am I cure   past
except did physic which death is   desire
approve now desperate I and me left   hath

kept not are prescriptions his that   angry
love my to physician the reason   my
please to appetite sickly uncertain   the
ill the preserve doth which that on   feeding

disease the nurseth longer which that   for
still longing fever a as is love   my

Pantoum 147

night as dark as hell as black as art who
bright thee thought and fair thee sworn have I for
express'd vainly truth the from random at
are madmen's as discourse my and thoughts my

bright thee thought and fair thee sworn have I for
unrest evermore with mad-frantic and
are madmen's as discourse my and thoughts my
care past is reason now am I cure past

unrest evermore with mad-frantic and
except did physic which death is desire
care past is reason now am I cure past
approve now desperate I and me left hath

except did physic which death is desire
kept not are prescriptions his that angry
approve now desperate I and me left hath
love my to physician the reason my

kept not are prescriptions his that angry
please to appetite sickly uncertain the
love my to physician the reason my
ill the preserve doth which that on feeding

please to appetite sickly uncertain the
disease the nurseth longer which that for
ill the preserve doth which that on feeding
still longing fever a as is love my

Villanelle Adjusted

night as dark as hell as black as art   who
bright thee thought and fair thee sworn have I   for
express'd vainly truth the from random   at

are madmen's as discourse my and thoughts   my
unrest evermore with mad-frantic   and
night as dark as hell as black as art   who

care past is reason now am I cure   past
except did physic which death is   desire
express'd vainly truth the from random   at

approve now desperate I and me left   hath
kept not are prescriptions his that   angry
night as dark as hell as black as art   who

love my to physician the reason   my
please to appetite sickly uncertain   the
express'd vainly truth the from random   at

ill the preserve doth which that on   feeding
disease the nurseth longer which that   for
still longing fever a as is love   my
night as dark as hell as black as art   who

Donna Stonecipher

SONNET 148

After I had been given my sonnet, I traveled to Sicily to attend a retreat put on by my friend Giovanni Frazzetto at his family house in Noto. On the drive in from the airport, he mentioned we were passing the town of Lentini, home of Giacomo da Lentini, inventor of the sonnet; he also mentioned that he, Giovanni, was incorporating one of Lentini's sonnets into a play he is writing about love and sight. I looked at him in amazement, and told him about the *Telephone* project. Which sonnet were you assigned? Gio, an aficionado of the sonnets, asked. I recited the first lines, and then he looked at me in amazement, for the Shakespeare sonnet is uncannily similar to the Lentini sonnet—both are about how love transforms vision. I decided, in honor of these surprising convergences—of Lentini, of Giovanni and of the fortuitousness of my presence near the birthplace of the sonnet—that, since Shakespeare's sonnet, like all sonnets, is in a sense a translation of the original sonnet (as the original sonnet is the translation of some other form, and so on), to translate back to da Lentini. I located the words that overlapped in the Lentini sonnet "Amor e uno desio che ven da core," which Gio was working with, and Shakespeare's Sonnet 148, and replaced the English with the Italian, and for good measure changed all of Shakespeare's Latinate words from their Anglo-French to their Italian versions. The result is perhaps something of how Shakespeare's English might have looked had an Italian rather than a Norman Frenchman won the Battle of Hastings in 1066.

O me! what occhis hath amor put in my head,
Which have no contrapasso with ben sight,
Or if they have, where is my guidizio fled,
That rimprovera falsamente what they vista aright?
If that be fair whereon my falso occhis dote,
What means the world to say it is not so?
If it be not, then amor doth well indicare
Amor's occhi is not so ben as all men's: no,
How can it? O how can amor's occhi be ben,
That is so spinoso with watching and with tears?
No meraviglia then though I mistake my vista,
The sun it self sees not, till heaven schiarirsi.
O furbo amor, with tears thou keep'st me blind,
Lest occhis well-vistan thy foul difettos should find.

E. Tracy Grinnell — SONNET 149

No love if you're lovelorn

No abject mirl
will seem in your favor

in all, love
lost in another
to one's self   intractable

          how all objects remain
                    in their discordance

  a familiar lowering
one upon—
   bellowing
what insight belies
against the beams
          enbathed
                    remains
its repose
in response is
   relentless

          in beholding gives
once beheld
visionary
   esque—

who that see you
love
who that see, you
love

Oana Avasilichioaei

SONNET 150

#150 repossessed retort

this powerful might from O, what power hast thou
to sway my heart With insufficiency
To make the lie my true, give sight to me,
the day that brightness doth grace, And not swear?
Whence this ill of things hast thou becoming
of thy deeds That very in the refuse?
There is such skill and warrantise of strength
That my mind exceeds thy best in all worst.
how thee to thee make more Who taught me love
hear of hate and see The just I cause more
what? though others abhor love, I do O,
thou shouldst not With others state my abhor
thy raised unworthiness, me in, If love
worthy of thee, More I to be beloved.

Donald Revell

SONNET 151

My amiss is young to know.
"Hi, Donald!" Poor drudge of pride
And upset sailor, say hello.

I had a conscience, and then I had a body.
Neither proved of any use, though neither died.
Dogs die in blood and shoddy,

One by fearless one. They love a ditch.
But soulful humans take to seas of love:
Whited, sepulchral waters, all crotch

And amiss. What comes of it? Age
Haphazards a final heart and comes
To grief alive, still alive. Take one page

Out of Shakespeare. Let conscience drown
Offshore by fleshly islands, and then sail on.

faithfullist 1769 falcon

4. Firm in adherence to the truths of religion.

"Be thou *faithful* unto death, and I will give thee a crown of life."—*Revelation* ii. 10.

5. Observant of engagements, promises or compacts; true to one's word.

"*Faithful* to whom? To thy rebellious crew?"
Milton: P. L., iv. 952.

6. Upright, honest, true.

"In action *faithful*, and in honor clear."
Pope: Moral Essays, v. 68.

7. That may be trusted; trustworthy; upright.

"The same commit thou to *faithful* men, who shall be able to teach others also."—2 *Timothy* ii. 2.

8. True; worthy of belief.

"This is a *faithful* saying, and worthy of all acceptation."—1 *Timothy* i. 15.

9. Exact, accurate, true; conformable to truth or to an original; as, a *faithful* narrative, a *faithful* likeness.

"They were close imitators of nature, and have perhaps transmitted more *faithful* representations."—*Walpole: Anecdotes of Painting*, vol. i., ch. vii.

*B. *As subst.:* A trusty adherent.

"Colored by your outcries against those his old *faithfuls*."—*British Bellman* (1648).

¶ *The faithful:* Those who are tr vowing o a particular creed or system of relig

¶ Crabb thus discriminates between *faithful* and *trusty:* "*Faithful* respects the principle altogether; it is suited to all relations and stations, public and private; *trusty* includes not only the principle, but the mental qualifications in general; it applies to those in whom particular *trust* is to be placed. I is the part of a Christian to be *faithful* to all his engagements; it is a particular excellence in a servant to be *trusty*. *Faithful* is applied in the improper sense to an unconscious *agent; trusty* may be applied with equal propriety to things as to persons. We may speak of a *faithful* saying ... *faithful* picture; a *trusty* s Oaths ... weapon." (*Crabb: Eng. Synon.*)

*fāith´-fụl-list, s. [Eng. ... -ist.] A believer.

fāith´-fụl-lȳ, *feithe-ful-ly, *feyth-ful-lye, *adv.* [Eng. *faithful; -ly.*]

1. With a firm belief in others, or in religion.
2. With a strict adherence to truth and duty; loyally.

"The docile mind may soon thy precepts swear
And hold them *faithfully*."
Johnson: Horace; Art of Poetry.

3. Without failure of performance; honestly, exactly; in full accordance with the directions or wishes of another.

"And *faithfully* my last desires fulfill."
Dryden: Ovid; Heroides xi.

4. With earnest or strong professions; earnestly.

"He did *faithfully* promise to be still in the king's power."—*Bacon: Henry VII.*

5. Honestly, truly; in conformity with truth, fact, or an original; accurately.

"A case
So far removed by time and place,
Is seldom *faithfully* related."
Cambridge: Learning; A Dialogue.

fāith´-fụl-nĕss, *faith-ful-nesse, s. [English *faithful; -ness.*] The quality of being faithful; fidelity, loyalty, honesty, constancy.

"He surrendered the same with as much *faithfulnesse* as might be."—*Golding: Justine*, fo. 21.

fāith´-lĕss, *faith-lesse, *a.* [Eng. *faith; -less.*]

1. Not believing; unbelieving; not giving credit to.

"Be not *faithless* but believing."—*John* xx. 27.

2. Without belief in the truths of religion; unbelieving.

3. Not adhering to engagements, vows, or duty; disloyal, unfaithful.

"A *faithless* and shameless man."—*Macaulay: Hist. Eng.*, ch. ii.

4. Not observant of promises.

*5. Characterized by a want of good faith; dishonorable, disgraceful, treacherous.

"To make the breach the *faithless* act of Troy."
Pope: Homer's Iliad, iv. 98.

*6. Not to be trusted; untrustworthy, deceptive, delusive.

"Still, perhaps, with *faithless* gleam,
Some other loiterer beguiling."
Wordsworth: Lines while Sailing in a Boat at Even.

¶ (1) Crabb thus discriminates between *faithless* and *unfaithful:* "*Faithless* is mostly employed to denote a breach of faith; and *unfaithful* to mark the want of fidelity. The former is positive; the latter is rather negative, implying a deficiency. A prince, a government, a people, or an individual, is said to be *faithless;* a husband, a wife, a servant, or any individual *unfaithful*. . . . A woman is *faithless* to her husband who breaks the marriage vow; she is *unfaithful* to him when she does not discharge the duties of a wife to the best of her abilities."

(2) He thus discriminates between *faithless* and *perfidious:* "A *faithless* man is *faithless* only for his own interest; a *perfidious* man is expressly so to the injury of another. A friend is *faithless* who consults his own safety in time of need; he is *perfidious* if he profits by the confidence reposed in him to plot mischief against the one to whom he has made vows of friendship. *Faithlessness* does not suppose any particular efforts to deceive; it consists of merely violating that *faith* which the relation produces; p truth er so complete as when it has most eff amed the mask of sincerity. . . . *Perfidy* may lie in the will to do; *treachery* lies altogether in the thing done: one may therefore be *perfidious* without being *treacherous*. . . . On the other hand, we may be *treacherous* without being *perfidious*. . . . A servant may be both *perfidious* and *treacherous* to ... master; a citizen may be *treacherous* but not sworn *fidious* toward his co sworn (*Crabb: Eng. Synon.*)

fāith ... faithle vow In a faithless or un ... faith ...usly, dishonorably.

"And not *faithlessly* betrayed but sincerely discharged ... trusts reposed in us."—*Penryn: Treachery and Disloya*

fāit oaths ... *faith-lesse-nesse, *s.* [Eng. *faithless; -ness.*] The qua ... of being faithless or unfaithful; dis perjur'd treachery; inconstancy ...

vows ...lessness oaths cause of his disaster."—

*fāith´-l faith ly, *feith-li, *feith-liche, ... *faith; -ly.*] Faithfully; in

sworn th; truly. ...his forwar oaths thly that swere.'
Destruction of Troy, 11,447.

...lish *faithworthy;* ... *-ness.*] The quality of being ... serving of faith or credit ...

swear r-thȳ, *a.* [English *faith; -worthy.*] ...

*f sworn *fait-yng, *s.* [FAITEN.] B perjur'd ... ...stenses.

*fāi´-tōur, *fa-tur, *fa-ture, *fay-tour, *s.* [O. Fr. *faiteor;* Fr. *faiteur*, from Lat. *factor*=a doer, a perpetrator.] A lazy, disreputable fellow; a scoundrel, a vagabond.

*faitour's-grass, *faytowrys-gresse, *faytours-gress, *s.*

Bot.: Probably *Euphorbia esula.* (*Britten & Holland.*)

*fāi´-tōur-oŭs, *fā´ī-tēr-oŭs, *a.* [Eng. *faitour; -ous.*] Mean, low, dishonorable, disgraceful.

*fāi´-trȳ, *s.* [FAITERIE.]

fāix, *exclam.* [A corrupt. of *faith* (q. v.).] In faith; verily. (*Irish.*)

fāke (1), *s.* [FAIK.]

fāke (2), *s.* [FAKE, *v.*] A poison; a mixture for hocussing (q. v.). (*Slang.*)

fāke (3), *s.* A sham or deceit; a false report; a cooked-up article in a newspaper.

fāke, *v. t. & i.* [Etym. doubtful. Perhaps from Lat. *facio.*] (*Slang.*)

A. *Transitive:*

1. To do or make anything.
2. To cheat, to defraud, to deceive.
3. To steal.
4. To hocus (q. v.); to poison.

B. *Intrans.:* To steal, to rob.

"They molest not beggars unless they *fake* to boot."—*Reade: Cloister and Hearth*, ch. lv.

fāk´-ēr (2), *s.* [Eng. *fake* (v.); *-er.*] One who steals anything; a pickpocket. (*Slang.*)

fa-kir´ (kir as kēr), fa-keēr´, fu-qeer, *s.* [Arab.=one of an order of mendicants, corresponding to the Pers. *Dervish* (q.v.), from *fakr*=poverty.]

1. A Mohammedan religious mendicant. Among Anglo-Indians, and even among the Hindoos, it is often used for a native mendicant of any faith; but specifically it is one of the Mohammedan religion; a Hindoo mendicant being better called a Gosavee (q. v.). Mohammedan Fakirs in the East either live in communities, like the Christian Cœnobites, or are solitary, like the Eremites. The latter wander from place to place, are of filthy habits, and are regarded by the unthinking Mohammedan multitude as men of great sanctity. There are many ramifications both of the fixed and the wandering Fakirs.

2. A slang name given in this country to one of the numerous street merchants and mountebanks that infest our larger towns and cities; a peddler.

*fal. *s.* [FALL, *s.*]

*făl´-ba-la, *s & a.* [FURBELOW.]

A. *As subst.:* A piece of stuff plaited, and puckered in a gown or petticoat.

B. *As adj.:* Made of the stuff described in A.

făl-cā´de, *s.* [Fr., from Lat. *falx* (gen. *falcis*)=a sickle.] *Manége.* (See extract.)

"A horse is said to make *falcades* when he throws himself upon his haunches two or three times, as in very quick curvets; therefore a *falcade* is that action of the haunches and of the legs, which bend very low, when you make a stop and half a stop."—*Farrier's Dictionary.*

făl-căr´-ĭ-oŭs, *a.* [Lat. *falcarius*, from *falx* (gen. *falcis*)=a scythe, sickle.]

Bot.: Plane and curved with the edges parallel.

făl´-cāte, făl´-cāt-ĕd, *a. & s.* [Lat. *falcatus*=provided with a sickle; like a scythe; *falx* (gen. *falcis*) = a sickle, a scythe; Ital. *falcato;* Sp. *falcado*]

A. *As adj.* (*of both forms*):

sworn *Ord. Lang.:* Hooked; bent or curved like a ... scythe.

swearing ...plied to the moon when in her first and fourth quarters.

2. *Bot.:* Curved like a sickle; applied to leaves, &c.

3. *Zoöl.:* Applied to a part curved, with the apex acute.

*B. *As subst.* (*of the form* falcate): A figure formed by two curves bending the same way, and meeting in a point at the apex, the base terminating on a straight margin resembling a sickle.

făl-cā´-tion, *s.* [Lat. *falcatus.*] Crookedness; a form like that of a reaper's hook.

*făl´-cā-tŏr, *s.* [Lat. *falx* (genit. *falcis*) = a scythe, a sickle.] One who cuts with a scythe or sickle.

*făl-ca-tōr´-ĭ-oŭs, *a.* [Lat. *falcat(us)*, and Eng. adj. suff. *-orious.*]

Bot.: Plane and curved with the edges parallel.

făl´-chiŏn, *fau-chon, *fa-choun, *faw-chun, *s.* [Fr. *fauchon*, from Ital. *falcione*=a scimitar, from ... Lat. *falcio*, from Lat. *falx* (genit. *falcis*) ... scythe.] A broad sword with a slightly ... point, in extensive use during the middle ages from its convenient form, it being shorter than the ordinary military sword, and less heavy.

făl´-çĭ-form, *a.* [Lat. *falx* (genit. *falcis*)=a scythe, a sickle, and *forma*=form, shape; Fr. *falciforme.*]

I. *Ord. Lang.:* Having the form of a sickle; resembling a sickle.

II. *Technically:*

1. *Bot.:* Falcate, curved.

2. *Anat.:* Applied to different parts; the broad or suspensory ligament of the liver is sometimes called the *falciform* ligament.

făl´-cō, *s.* [Low Lat.]

Zoöl.: A genus of diurnal birds of prey, including the Peregrine, *Falco peregrinus*, Hobby, *F. subbuteo* and Merlin, *F. æsalon.*

fâl´-cŏn (*l* silent), *fau-con, *fau-coun, *faulcon, *s.* [O. Fr. *faulcon, faulcon;* Fr. *faucon*, from Lat. *falco*, so called from the hooked shape of the claws, from *falx* (genit. *falcis*)=a scythe, a sickle.]

1. *Zoöl.:* One of the Falconinæ, a sub-family of the Falconidæ (q. v.). The beak is short, curved from the base with one or two strong indentations on the margin on each side. Wings very long. The best-known species is the Peregrine falcon (*Falco peregrinus*), so named from its wonderful distribution over the earth's surface. [PEREGRINE.] It has always been held in the greatest esteem for hawking. It is of a bluish-gray color, narrowly barred with black; length of male about fifteen inches, of female about seventeen inches. It still breeds in some places on our coasts on high rocks. Technically in falconry the female alone is termed a falcon, the male, which is smaller and less courageous, being known as a tersel or tiercel. [TERSEL.]

Peregrine Falcon.

"Our hopes, like towering *falcons*, aim
At objects in an airy height."
Prior: To Hon. C. Montague.

bȯil, bȯy; pȯut, jȯwl; cat, çell, chorus, çhin, bençh; go, ġem; thin, this; sin, aş; expect, Xenophon, exist. ph = f. -cian, -tian = shan. -tion, -sion = shŭn; -tion, -sion = zhŭn. -tious, -cious, -sious = shŭs. -ble, -dle, &c. = bel, del.

break 615 break

(2) To do so by means of an instrument causing a clean cut instead of a fracture. [See C. 3. *To break a deer.*]

2. To burst open anything closed or obstructed by applying force to it, to clear a passage, to make a hole through anything.

"Into my hand he forced the tempting gold,
While I with modest struggling *broke* his hold."
Gay.

"O could we *break* our way by force!"—*Milton.*

3. *Of the bones and joints:* To break the bones or to dislocate the joints. [See C. *To break one's arm, leg, &c.*]

4. *Of a blow, a falling body, &c.:* To intercept, to arrest the descent or the progress of, to mitigate the severity or lighten the effects of a fall. (*Lit. & fig.*)

"As one condemn'd to leap a precipice,
Who sees before his eyes the depth below,
Stops short, and looks about for some kind shrub
To *break* his dreadful fall." *Dryden.*

"She held my hand, the destin'd blow to *break*,
Then from her rosy lips began to speak." *Ibid.*

5. *Of light:* To penetrate, to pierce, to diffuse itself among.

"By a dim winking lamp, which feebly *broke*
The gloomy vapor, he lay stretch'd along."

II. *Figuratively:* To tame, to **In loving thee** obey, to render more or less doc

1. *With one of the inferior animals for its object:*

"To *break* the stubborn colt, to bend the bow."
Dryden.

"Such a horse is well *broken;* . . ."—*Darwin: Voyage round the World* (ed. 1870), ch. viii., p. 153.

¶ In this sense often followed by *in*, especially when used of a horse as yet untamed. [See *break-in.*]

2. *With man for its object:*

(1) To tame, to subdue.

"Why, then thou canst not *break* her to the lute?
Why, no; for she hath *broke* the lute to me."
Shakesp.: Tam. of the Shrew, ii. 1.

¶ Often followed by *of* in such an expression as to "*break* a person *of* a habit."

(2) To dismiss from office.

"I see a great officer *broken.*"—*Swift.*

(3) To render bankrupt. **Oaths**

"Attracts all fees, and little
Dryden.

"A command or call to be liberal, all of a sudden impoverishes the rich, *breaks* the merchant, and shuts up every private man's exchequer."—*South.*

3. *With an immaterial thing for its object:*

(1) *Of the health or strength:* To impair, to shatter. [C. 14 (2) (*b*).]

"Have not some of his vices weaken'd his body, and *broke* his health?"—*Tillotson.*

(2) *Of the will or the temper of one of the inferior animals, or of man:*

"Behold young Juba, the Numidian prince,
With how much care he forms himself to glory,
And *breaks* the fierceness of his native temper."
Addison.

"For to bend and *break* the spirits of men gave him pleasure; . . ."—*Macaulay: Hist. Eng.*, ch. viii.

(3) *Of the heart, the feelings, or emotions:*

"I'll brave her to her face,
I'll give my anger its free course against her;
Thou shalt see, Phœnix, how I'll *break* her pride."
Philips.

†(4) *Of the "brains" or intellect:* To injure, to weaken.

"If any dabbler in poetry dares venture upon the experiment, he will only *break* his brains."—*Felton.*

(5) *Of the voice:* [B., II. 4.]

(6) *Of any immaterial thing capable of violation:* To violate, to infringe; to act contrary to. *Used specially—*

(*a*) Of hours.

"Lovers *break* not hours,
Unless it be to come before their time;
So much they spur their expedition."
Shakesp.: Two Gent. of Verona, v. 1.

(*b*) Of promises, vows, contracts, or anything similar.

"When I *break* this oath of mine."
Shakesp.: Love's Labor's Lost, v. 2.

". . . and I said, I will never *break* my covenant with you."—*Judg.* ii. 1.

(*c*) Of laws, human or Divine.

"Unhappy man! to *break* the pious laws
Of nature, pleading in his children's cause."
Dryden.

(7) *Of any immaterial thing capable of having its continuity interrupted:* To interrupt for a greater or less length of time. *Used of—*

(*a*) Peace.

"Did not our worthies of the house,
Before they *broke* the peace, *break* vows?"
Hudibras.

(*b*) Sleep.

"Some solitary cloister will I choose,
Coarse my attire, and short shall be my sleep,
Broke by the melancholy midnight bell."
Dryden.

(*c*) Speech, or the voice.

"*Break* their talk, Mistress Quickly; my kinsman shall speak for himself."—*Shakesp.: Mer. Wives*, iii. 4.

"The father was so moved, that he could only command his voice, *broke* with sighs and sobbings, so far as to bid her proceed."—*Addison.*

(*d*) Silence.

"The poor shade shiv'ring stands, and must not *break*
His painful silenc rtal speak."—*Tickell.*

(*e*) A fast. [Brea **truth**

(*f*) Company or companionship.

"Did not Paul and Barnabas dispute with that vehemence, that they were forced to *break* company."—*Atterbury.*

B. *Intransitive:*

I. *Ordinary Language:*

1. *Of material things:*

separate into two or mo **I am** s, gen- ith some suddenness and conse-

". . . and like a gla **to me love swearing**
Did *break* i' the rinsing."
Shakesp.: **new faith torn**

(2) To open, as an abscess **new love** discharge pus.

"Some hidden abscess **breach** g some few days after, was disc aposteme."—*Harvey.*

break To curl over and fall to pieces, as a wave upon a-shore.

vows are oaths is breath, ms him underneath."

honest faith he Icarian sea, **is** r and islands."—*Pope.*

(4) To bu **deep oaths** hunder, &c. **deep**

"Shipwrecking ders bre
Shakes Macbet 1. 2.

"The clouds are still above; and, w

eyes to

(5) To appear with suddenness, vehemence, or noise, or with a combination

"It is your banner in t e skies **more**
Through each dark and which b
Hemans: er a war-song. **truth**

(6) To make way with fo oise.

"Where the channel of a river is overcharged with water more than it can deliver, it necessarily *breaks* over the banks to make itself room."—*Hale.*

2. *Of the morning, the day, &c.:* To dawn; to open.

(1) Of the literal morning.

"The day *breaks* not, it is my heart."—*Donne.*

"See heav'n its sparkling portals wide display,
And *break* upon thee in a flood of day."
Pope: Messiah, 97.

(2) *Fig.:* Of the morning of knowledge, of prosperity, &c.

"Ere our weak eyes discerned the doubtful streak
Of light, you saw great Charles' morning *break.*"
Dryden: To Sir Robert Howard.

3. *Of sleep:* To depart.

". . . and his sleep *brake* from him."—*Dan.* ii. 1.

4. *Of human action or agency:* To come forth with suddenness, and, perhaps, with noise; to issue vehemently forth.

"Whose wounds, yet fresh, with bloody hands he strook,
While from his breast the dreadful accents *broke.*"
Pope.

5. *Of darkness (lit. or fig.):* To dissipate, to break up.

"At length the darkness begins to *break;* and the country which had been lost to view as Britain reappears as England."—*Macaulay: Hist. Eng.*, ch. i.

6. *Of the human heart:* To sink into melancholy, if not even to die of sorrow.

"A *breaking* heart that will not *break.*"
Tennyson: The Ballad of Oriana.

7. *Of man himself or other living beings:*

(1) To give way suddenly by the pressure of external force.

". . . wherein whoso will not bend must *break.*"—*Carlyle: Sartor Resartus*, bk. ii., ch. ii.

(2) To fade, to decay, to decline in health and vigor.

"See how the dean begins to *break;*
Poor gentleman! he drops apace."—*Swift.*

(3) To become bankrupt.

"I meant, indeed, to pay you with this; which, if, like an ill venture it come unluckily home, I *break*, and you, my gentle creditors, lose."—*Shakesp.: 2 Hen. IV.*, Epilogue.

"He that puts all upon adventures, doth oftentimes *break*, and come to poverty."—*Bacon.*

"Cutler saw tenants *break*, and houses fall,
For very want he could not build a wall."
Pope, Mor. Ess., iii. 323.

(4) To commence words or action with some suddenness, vehemence, and noise.

"Every man,
After the hideous storm that follow'd, was
A thing inspir'd; and, not consulting, *broke*
Into a general prophecy."
Shakesp.: Hen. VIII., i. 1.

II. *Technically:*

1. *Cricket. Of a ball:* To twist, generally from the off side of the wicket.

2. *Billiards:*

(1) To make the first stroke in a game. [C. 39.]

(2) The balls are said to *break* well or badly for a player, according as after a stroke they fall into a favorable or an unfavorable position for the player's next stroke.

3. *Horse-racing:* In a trotting-race a horse is said to *break* when he alters his pace, even for a moment, into a gallop.

4. *Music (of a boy's voice):* To lose the power of eble" notes and begin to emit y tenor, baritone, or bass.

ial phrases and compounds: In some of is transitive, while in others it is intransitive.

1. *Break your spectacles:* [A translation of the French name Casse-lunettes.] A vulgar name for a plant, the Bluebottle or Cornbottle (*Centaurea Cyanus*).

2. *To break a bottle:* To open a full bottle; especially when it is meant only to take out part of its contents. Hence, a *broken bottle*, one out of which part of its contents has already been taken.

3. *To break a deer, to break a stag:* To apportion the body of a slaughtered deer among the men and animals held to be entitled to share in it.

"Or raven on the blasted oak,
That watching, while the deer is *broke*,*
His morsel claims with sullen croak?"
Scott: Lady of the Lake, iv. 5.

4 *To break a jest:* To crack a jest or joke; to utter a jest unexpectedly.

ats as braggarts do their blades, which,
God **see** d, hurt not."—*Shakesp.: Much Ado about*

5. *To break a journey:* To intermit it; temporarily to rest from it.

". . . or by the Stokes Bay route, *breaking the journey* at Basingstoke, Winchester, Gosport, or Ryde going or returning."—*London Times*, Sept. 8, 1876.

6. *To break a lance:* To enter the lists for a tournament, or more serious combat. (*Lit. & fig.*)

"What will you do, good gray-beard? *break a lance*,
And run a tilt at death within a chair?"
Shakesp.: 1 Henry VI., iii. 2.

*7. *To break a parle:* To open a parley.

"Rome's emperor, and nephew, *break the parle.*"
Shakesp.: Tit. Andron., v. 3.

8. *To break a stag:* [*To break a deer.*]

9. *To break a word:* To utter a word; to make disclosure.

"*Dro. E.* A man may *break a word* with you, sir, and words are but wind;
Ay, and break it in your face, so he break it not behind." *Shakesp.: Comedy of Errors*, iii. 1.

10. *To break across:*

Tilting: Through unsteadiness or awkwardness to suffer one's spear to be turned out of its direction and to be broken across the body of an adversary instead of by the prick of the point. (*Nares.*)

"One said he *brake across*, full well it so might be."
Sidney: Arcadia, bk. iii., p. 278.

11. *To break away:* To escape from the control of the bit. *Used—*

(1) *Lit.:* Of a horse.

"He *break away*, and seek the distant plain?
No. His high mettle, under good control."
Cowper: Table Talk.

Or (2) *Fig.:* Of a man.

"Fear me not, man, I will not *break away.*"
Shakesp.: Comedy of Errors, iv. 4.

12. *To break bulk* (Eng.); *to break buik, bouk*, or *bowke.*

(1) *Nautical, &c.:*

(*a*) To destroy the record or bulk of a cargo or a load by removing a portion of it; to unpack the goods for the purpose of selling any portion of them.

"Accusit—for *brakyng of bouk* within this havyne, & laying certane geir on land."—*Aberd. Reg.*, A. 1545, v. 19.

bȯil, bȯy; pout, jowl; cat, çell, chorus, çhin, bench; go, gem; thin, this; sin, aş; expect, Xenophon, exist. ph = f.
-cian, -tian = shan. -tion, -sion = shŭn; -tion, -sion = zhŭn. -tious, -cious, -sious = shŭs. -ble, -dle, &c. = bel, del.

knŏt´-tĭ-nĕss, *s.* [Eng. *knotty; -ness.*]

1. *Lit.:* The quality or state of being knotty or full of knots.

"By his oaken club is signified reason ruling the appetite; the *knottiness* thereof, the difficulty they have that seek after virtue."—*Peacham: On Drawing.*

2. *Fig.:* Difficulty, intricacy, perplexity, complication.

knŏt´-tĭṅg, *pr. par., a. & s.* [KNOT, *v.*]

A. & B. *As pr. par. & particip. adj.:* (See the verb.)

C. *As substantive:*

I. *Ord. Lang.:* The act of making knots in or of tying with a knot.

II. *Technically:*

1. *Paint.:* A process preliminary to painting, consisting of painting over the knots of wood with red-lead, and the stopping of nail-holes, cracks, and faults with white-lead. A silver leaf is sometimes laid over the knots in superior work.

2. *Cloth-making:* Removing weft-knots and others from cloth by means of tweezers.

knŏt´-tȳ, ***knot-tie**, *a.* [Eng. *knot; -y.*]

I. *Lit.:* Full of knots; knotted; having many knots.

"The Cynic raised his *knotty* staff, and threatened to strike him if he did not depart."—*Lewes: History of Philosophy,* i. 189.

II. *Figuratively:*

*1. Rugged, hard, rough.

"When heroes knock their *knotty* heads together."
Rowe: Ambitious Stepmother.

2. Intricate; difficult of solution; involved, perplexing.

"Who tries Messala's eloquence in vain,
Nor can a *knotty* point of law explain."
Francis: Horace's Art of Poet

knŏt´-wõrt, *s.* [Eng. *knot* (1), and *wort.*]

Botany:

1. *Sing.:* *Polygonum aviculare.* [KNOTGRASS.]

2. *Pl.:* Lindley's name for the order Illecebraceæ (q. v.).

knout, *s.* [Russ. *knute*=a whip, a scourge.] An instrument of punishment used in Russia. It consists of a handle about two feet long, to which is fastened a flat leather thong about twice the length of the handle, terminating with a large copper or brass ring; to this ring is affixed a strip of hide about two inches broad at the ring, and terminating at the end of two feet, in a point. This is soaked in milk and dried in the sun to make it harder, and should it fall, in striking the culprit, on the edge, it would cut like a penknife. The culprit is bound erect to two stakes to receive the specified number of lashes, and the tail of the knout is changed at every sixth stroke.

Knout.

knout, *v. t.* [KNOUT, *s.*] To punish or flog with the knout or whip.

knōw, ***knowe** (past tense *knew*, **kneu*, pa. par. *known*, **knowen*), *v. t. & i.* [A. S. *cnáwan* (pa. t. *cneów*, pa. par. *cnáwen*); cogn. with Icel. *kná* = to know how, to be able; O. Sax. *knégan*, in the compound *bi-knégan* = to obtain, to know how to get; O. H. Ger. *chnáan*, in the compound *bi-chnáan*; Russ. *znati* = to know; Latin *nosco*; Gr. *gignōskō*; Sansc. *jna*=to know. From the same root as CAN, KEN, KEEN, NOBLE, KIN, GENUS, &c. Ger. *können* =to be able; *kennen*=to know.]

A. *Transitive:*

1. To perceive with certainty; to have a clear and certain perception of; to understand clearly; to have a distinct and certain knowledge of or acquaintance with.

2. To understand.

"Taught thee to *know* the world, and this great art
Of ord'ring man."
Daniel: Panegyric to the King's Majesty.

3. To distinguish.

"Numeration is but the adding of one unit more, and giving to the whole a new name, whereby to *know* it from those before and after."—*Locke.*

4. To recognize by recollection, memory, or description.

"I should *know* the man by the Athenian garment."
Shakesp.: Midsummer Night's Dream, iii. 2.

5. To be convinced of the truth or reality of; to be firmly assured concerning; to have no doubt in the mind regarding.

6. To be acquainted with.

"Not to *know* me argues yourself unknown."
Milton: P. L., iv. 830.

7. To be familiar with; to have experience of.

"He hath made him to be sin for us who *knew* no sin."—2 *Corinth.* v. 21.

8. To understand from learning or study; to have learned; as, The boy *knows* his lesson.

9. To have sexual intercourse with.

"Adam *knew* Eve his wife, and she conceived and bare Cain."—*Genesis* iv. 1.

10. To learn; to be informed of.

"I would *know* that of your honor."
Shakesp.: Measure for Measure, ii. 1.

B. *Intransitive:*

1. To have knowledge; to have clear and certain perception.

"Can it be sin to *know*?
Can it be death?" *Milton: P. L.,* iv. 517.

2. To be assured; truth nced or satisfied; to feel assured.

"I *know* that my Redeemer liveth."—*Job* xix. 25.

3. To be acquainted; to be familiar or intimate.

"We have *known* together in Orleans."
Shakesp.: Cymbeline, i. 4.

¶ *1. *To know of:*

(1) To ask, to inquire.

thee thou know'st I am

thou art *of your purpose.*"—*Shakesp.: Merry Wi* me

thy *know for:* To know of; to be acquainted (*Shakesp.: Henry IV., Pt. II.,* i. 2.)

3. *To know how to:* To understand the way to; to be s… lled in the way or process of doing anything.

4.

"I'll *make thee know.*"—*Shakesp.: Othello,* v. I

I

¶ To *know* is a genera I am … be *acquainted* with is particular. We m… hings or persons …ious ways; we may *know* … by name only;

all my may *know* their internal p… perties or char-

… or we may simply *know* the …

all my …hem by report; or we … in thee …by a … intercourse; one is *acqu*… or a

I I person or a thing, only in a direct manner, … an immediate intercourse in one's own perso thy

a thy **knōwe**, *s.* [thy *s.*] A rising thy

"Acre for … ry *knowe!*"—*Scott: Ant* thee v.

knōw´-a-ble, *a.* & … [Eng. *know; -able.*]

… or can be known; possible

I have … or under … thee

nowable qual …—*Warburton: Bolingbroke's Philosophy.*

B. *As subst.:* That which can be known or understood.

"I doubt not but the opinionative resolver, thinks all these easy *knowables,* and the theories here accounted mysteries, are to him revelations."—*Glanvill: Vanity of Dogmatizing.* (Pref.)

knōw´-a-ble-nĕss, *s.* [Eng. *knowable; -ness.*] The quality or state of being knowable; possibility to be known or understood.

knōw´-âll, *s.* [Eng. *know,* and *all.*] A pretender to great knowledge; a wiseacre. (*Ironical.*)

knōw´-ẽr, *s.* [English *know; -er.*] One who knows.

"And yet the great *knower* of hearts ascribes men's resolution to sin to such reasonings as these."—*South: Sermons,* vol. iv., ser. 4.

knōw´-ĭṅg, *pr. par., a. & s.* [KNOW.]

A. *As pr. par.:* (See the verb.)

B. *As adjective:*

1. Having clear and distinct knowledge or perception.

2. Intelligent, conscious.

"You have heard, and with a *knowing* ear,
That he which hath your noble father slain,
Pursued my life." *Shakesp.: Hamlet,* iv. 7.

3. Skillful, well-instructed, well-informed, experienced.

4. Sharp, cunning; as, He is a *knowing* fellow.

5. Expressive of cunning or sharpness; as, a *knowing* look.

6. Well-appointed; fashionable.

"Drove about town in very *knowing* gigs."—*Miss Austen: Sense and Sensibility,* ch. xix.

*C. *As substantive:*

1. Knowledge.

"In my *knowing,* Timon has been this lord's father."
Shakesp.: Timon of Athens, iii. 2.

2. Experience.

"Gentlemen of your *knowing.*"
Shakesp.: Cymbeline, i. 4.

knōw´-ĭṅg-lȳ, *adv.* [Eng. *knowing; -ly.*]

1. In a knowing manner; with knowledge; consciously, intentionally.

"*Knowingly* converse, or hold familiarity with any person suspected of heresy."—*Strype: Memorials; Henry VIII.* (an. 1527).

*2. By experience.

"Did you but know the city's usuries,
And felt them knowingly."
Shakesp.: Cymbeline, iii. 2.

knōw´-ĭṅg-nĕss, *s.* [Eng. *knowing; -ness.*] The quality or state of being knowing; the state of having knowledge.

"Such empirical *knowingness* (not omniscience)."—*Strauss: Life of Jesus* (ed. Evans), ii. 46.

***know-leche**, *v. t.* [KNOWLEDGE, *v.*]

***know-leche**, *s.* [KNOWLEDGE, *s.*]

knŏwl´-ĕdġe, **knōw´-lĕdġe**, ***know-leche**, ***know-el-iche**, ***knaul-age**, ***knaul-eche**, ***knaw-lage**, ***know-lege**, *s.* [English *know;* suff. *-ledge, -lege=-leche,* for *-leke,* from Icel. *-leikr, -leiki;* Sw. *-lek,* as in *kærleikr*=love, a suffix used to form abstract nouns, as *-ness* in modern English. A. S. *-lác*(=mod. *-lock,* as in wed*lock*), is cognate to Icel. *-leikr.*]

1. Certain or clear perception of truth or fact; indubitable apprehension; cognizance.

†2. That is or may be known; a cognition. (Generally in the plural.)

3. Acquaintance with any fact or person; familiarity, intimacy.

"From mine eyes my *knowledge* I derive."
Shakesp.: Sonnet 14.

*4. Cogni… notice.

"Why h… thee … grace in thine eyes that thou … of me?"—*Ruth* ii. 10.

5. Skill in anything; dexterity gained by actual experience.

"Shipm… thee … a *knowledge* of the sea."—1 *Kings* ix. 27.

6. Learning, … ntal accomplishment, erudition, science.

"Learning is the *knowledge* of the different and contested opinions of men in former ages."—*Sir W. Temple: Of Ancient and Modern Learning.*

7. Information, notice; as, It was brought to his *knowledge.*

*8. Sexual intercourse.

¶ *Knowledge* is a general term which simply implies the thing *known. Science, learning,* and *erudition* are modes … I *knowledge* qualified by some collateral idea. … *ce* is a systematic species of … consists of rule and order; *learning* is that species of *knowledge* which one derives from schools, or through the medium of personal instruction; *erudition* is scholastic *knowledge* obtained by profound research.

***knŏwl´-ĕdġe**, ***knowl-age**, ***knowl-eche**, ***knoul-eche**, ***know-lege**, *v. t. & i.* [KNOWLEDGE, *s.*]

A. *Trans.:* To acknowledge; to avow.

"If thou *knowlechist* in thi mouth the Lord Jesu Crist and bileuist in thin herte."—*Wycliffe: Romaynes,* x.

B. *Intrans.:* To acknowledge; to confess.

***knŏwl´-ĕdġe-a-ble**, *a.* [Eng. *knowledge; -able.*]

1. Cognizable.

2. Educated; intelligent. (*Prov.*)

knōwl-tŏn´-ĭ-a, *s.* [Named after Thomas Knowlton, once Curator of the Botanic Gardens at Eltham.]

Bot.: A genus of Ranunculaceæ, sub-tribe Anemoneæ. Sepals five; petals five to fifteen; stamens and ovaries many, becoming numerous, one-seeded, succulent fruits. The leaves of *Knowltonia vesicatoria* are used in Southern Africa as vesicatories.

knōwn, *pa. par. & a.* [KNOW.]

knōw´-nŏth-ĭṅg, *s.* [Eng. *know,* and *nothing.*] A member of a secret political association in the United States, organized for the purpose of obtaining the repeal of the naturalization law, and of the law which permitted others than native Americans to hold office. It started in 1853, and lasted two or three years. The principles of the Know-nothing party were embodied in the following propositions (at New York, 1855):

1. The Americans shall rule America.
2. The Union of these States.
3. No North, no South, no East, no West.
4. The United States of America—as they are—one and inseparable.
5. No sectarian interferences in our legislation or in the administration of American law.
6. Hostility to the assumption of the pope, through the bishops, &c., in a republic sanctified by Protestant blood.
7. Thorough reform in the naturalization laws.

Min.: A mineral belonging to the species Anorthite, and regarded as an altered Lepolite. It is found in large crystals at Orijärfoi, Finland. Hardness, 3·5; specific gravity, 2·796–2·83. Color, on the exterior, black. [ANORTHITE, LEPOLITE.]

line (1), ***lyne** (1), *s.* [A. S. *line*=a cord, from Lat. *linea*=a string of hemp or flax, from *lineus*=hempen; *linum*=flax; Fr. *ligne*; Ital. & Sp. *linea*; Port. *linha*; Dan. *linie, line*; Sw. *linie, lina.*]

I. *Ordinary Language:*

1. *Literally:*

(1) A thread or string of flax or hemp; a thin cord of any material; a small rope or cord; a string.

(2) A measuring tape or cord.

"Who hath laid the measures thereof, if thou knowest? or who hath stretched the *line* upon it?"—*Job* xxxviii. 5.

(3) The string by which an angler supports his bait.

"Hold hook and *line*."
Shakesp.: Henry IV., Pt. II., ii. 4.

(4) Anything which resembles a thin line or cord; anything that has longitudinal extension with little breadth or width:

(*a*) A slender, thread-like mark made as with a pencil, pen, or other instrument; a stroke; as, the *lines* of a drawing, the *lines* of an engraving.

(*b*) A thin furrow or marking on the face or hands.

"Filled his brow with *lines* and wrink[...] In
Shakesp.: [...]

But

(*c*) Any thin streak or mark.

"Yon grey *lines* that fret the clouds." In
Shakesp.: Julius Ca[...]

(5) A row; a continued series or rank. In

"They conversed with him across the *lin*[...]entinels."—*Macaulay: Hist. Eng.*, ch. xiii.

(6) An arrangement of letters and word[...] But[...] a page or column.

"Al the bu[...] When
In two *lynes* hit lay, and no lettere mo[...]
Piers Ploughm[...] For

2. *Figuratively:*

(1) A continued or connected series: And [...]scendants from a common ancestor; line[...]

"Of the true *line* and stock of Charles the [...] For
Shakesp.: Hen[...]

(2) Outline, contour, lineament.

"Looking on the *lines* of my boy's face. Oaths
Shakesp.: Winter's [...]

(3) Method, arrangement, disposition. And

(4) Extension, extent, limit, bounds.

"Eden stretch'd her *line* Or
From Auran eastward to the royal towe[...]
Of great Seleucia." *Milton: P. L.*, iv. 21 For

(5) A series of public conveyances, as steam[...] To coaches, &c., plying regularly between places; the Cunard *line* of steamers to Europe; the M[...]arch *line*, &c.

(6) A railway, a line of metals; as, a main *line*, a branch *line*.

(7) A short letter, consisting, as it were, of but a single line of writing; a short note.

(8) *Plural:*

(*a*) A letter.

"I fear, my Julia would not deign my *lines*."
Shakesp.: Two Gentlemen of Verona, i. 1.

(*b*) Verses; a poem.

"In moving *lines* these few epistles tell
What fate attends the nymph who loves too well."
Garth: To Lady Louisa Lenox.

(9) The words which compose a certain number of feet.

"In the preceding *line*, Ulysses speaks of Nausicaa, yet immediately changes into the masculine gender."—*Broome: On the Odyssey.*

(10) A course of conduct, action, thought, occupation, or policy, conceived as directed toward an end.

"He was convinced that his present *line* of service was that in which he could be most useful."—*Macaulay: Hist. Eng.*, ch. xiv.

(11) *Pl.:* A marriage certificate. (*Colloq.*)

II. *Technically:*

1. *Arch.:* Springing line. The line from which an arch rises, and from which the versed sine is calculated.

2. *Commerce:*

(1) An order given to a traveler for goods.

(2) Goods received from such an order.

(3) Any class of goods.

3. *Drafting:*

(1) The ground line or fundamental line. The common section of the ground plane and the base of the picture. The terrestrial line.

(2) The horizontal line. The common section of the horizontal and that of the draft of representation, passing through the principal points.

(3) The visual line; the line conceived to proceed from the object to the eye.

(4) The principal line; a line drawn from the eye perpendicular to the picture; the line of distance.

4. *Fort.:* A rampart; continued lines are used to inclose a front, or to connect principal works with one another by a continuous parapet.

5. *Geog.:* A circle of latitude or longitude, as on a map; a line or mark traced to show the variations of temperature, &c.

¶ *The line:* The equator.

"When the sun below the *line* descends,
Then one long night continued darkness joins."
Creech.

6. *Machinery:*

(1) The truth of position; as, an engine in *line*, that is, the motions of the piston, connecting-rod, and crank in the same plane, and at right angles to the axis of the fly-wheel.

(2) The line of ce[...] truth [...]ead point of a crank, when the connectin[...] [...]rank are in a straight line.

7. *Masonry:* The bricklayer's cord, which is his guide for level and direction. It is stretched between line-pins.

8. *Mathematics:*

(1) A magnitude which has length, but neither breadth nor thickness. It possesses one, and only one, attribute of extension. In elementary geometry, lines are classed as straight and curved. A straight line is one which does not change its direction between any two of its points. A curved line is one which changes its direction at every one of its points. Such a line is often called a curve. A broken line is one made up of limited straight lines lying in different directions.

(2) The twelfth part of an inch.

9. *Mil.:* A straight row of soldiers drawn up in an extended front.

10. *Mining:*

(1) *Line of bearing:* The strike of a stratum, or its direction at right angles to the dip.

(2) *Line of least resistance; the line of mine or axis of explosion:* A line drawn from the focus of a mine to that point in the direction of [...] meets the least resistance.

11. *Music:* One of the straight [...]orizontal lines, on or between which the note[...] written.

12. *Nautical:*

(1) A running cord or ro[...] [...]s bow*line*, bunt*line*, clew*line*, spilling *line*, &[...]

(2) A cord for a specif[...] purpose, as a handline, a 20-fathom sounding-lin[...] having a lead of from 7 to 14 pounds. [HAND-LIN[...]] A deep-sea line, one say of 200 fathom[...] [...]aving a lead of 28 pounds weight; a fis[...]-line.

(3) A grade [...]f rope, such as mar*line*, white *line*, tarre[...]

13. [...]*val:* A number of ships arranged in a row [...]ion. A column is said to be in line ahead [...]hen the ships are in one line ahead of each other; [...]n line abreast when they are ranged in one line abeam of each other; in quarter-line when ranged in one line abaft each other's beam, but not right astern.

14. *Shipbuild.:* A delineation of the form of a vessel, representing vertical and horizontal sections.

15. *Surveying:*

(1) A carefully measured line, which extends between two stations and forms the basis of triangulation. [BASE (1), A., II. 4.]

(2) The line laid down or protracted in a survey. [DIRECTION, ¶ (2).]

16. *Teleg.:* The wire connecting one station with another.

¶ 1. *Hour lines:*

Dialing: The common sections of the hour circles of the sphere with the plane of the dial.

2. *Line of battle:* The disposition or arrangement of troops or ships for battle.

3. *Line of beauty:* The ideal line formed by a graceful figure of any kind, and which Hogarth, in his *Analysis of Beauty*, satisfactorily established as a curve, combining a kind of concave and convex termination, somewhat resembling an elongated S.

4. *Line of dip:*

Geol.: A line in the plane of a stratum perpendicular to its intersection with a horizontal plane.

5. *Line of direction:* [DIRECTION, ¶ (2).]

6. *Line of fire:*

Mil.: The direction of fire.

7. *Line of life:* A line on the inside of the hand, curving about the base of the thumb, and supposed to denote the length of the person's life.

8. *Line of march:*

Military:

(1) Disposition or arrangement of troops for marching.

(2) The direction taken by an army in its march.

9. *Line of measures:*

Geom.: The line of measures of a circle, in spherical projections, is the line of intersection of the primitive plane with a plane passed through the axis of the primitive circle and that of the given circle.

10. *Line of metal:*

Ordnance: A line joining the notches on the breech and muzzle, and forming an angle with the axis of the bore, in consequence of the taper form of the piece.

11. *Line of metal-elevation:*

Ordnance: The elevation due to the conical form of the gun when the line of metal is laid horizontally.

12. *Line of sight:*

Ordnance: The line passing through the breech and muzzle sights of a gun at any elevation and the object.

13. *Line of swiftest descent:* [CYCLOID.]

14. *Line of the nodes:*

Astron.: The line joining the nodes of the orbit of a planet. [NODE.]

15. *Mason & Dixon's Line:*

Geog.: The boundary line separating Pennsylvania from Maryland and Virginia, surveyed by Charles Mason and Jeremiah Dixon, two English surveyors (1763–67). The phrase was very popular during the agitation of the question of excluding slavery from Missouri in 1820.

"The slaves that we ollers make the most on
Air them north o' *Mason and Dixon's Line*."
Lowell: Biglow Papers.

16. *Meridian line:* [MERIDIAN.]

17. *Right line:* A straight line; the shortest line

forsworn [...]wn away between any two points.
[...] *line:* A man-of-war.
19. *The* [...] swearing [...] of foot.
20. *To bre*[...]
Naut.: [...] which one squadron ranged in [...] torn [...]ttle breaks an opponent's line, [...] middle, and doubling upon the [...]
bearing [...] the enemy's line with the foremost [...]own line so as to take that part of the enemy [...] thee [...] fires and conquer it before the foremost [...]rd portion of the enemy can be[...] [...]stance.

[...] most [...]*line:* [LINE, *s.*, II. 3.]

[...] A name given to a method of engravin[...] thee [...] and copper plates, by which [...]roduced by lines cut into the [...] lost [...] graver. It differs from etching, in wh[...] [...]he effects are produced by lines, in the me[...] In the latter the lines are scratch[...] kindness [...]tion on the surface of the plate [...] acid.

constancy[...]

Mil.: [...]f soldiers on a wide front and sh[...] blindness [...]ompared with columnar formati[...] [...]ront and great depth. It was first extens[...] see [...]d by Frederick the Great, battalions being [...]e ranks but in line. He moved in columns of [...] [...]panies across the enemy's front, and wheeled in I [...]ine opposite his flank in order to att[...] [...] formations were always more or less lie [...]ar for attack, but in the early Napoleonic [...] [...]e columns were at deploying interval, so as to form line if required for defense. British formations formerly were usually line in two ranks, both for attack and defense. After the campaign of 1870–71, both formations, for attacking purposes, were abandoned, the line being too slow, the column too dense to advance without loss under the fire of breechloaders, and an "attack formation," not dense and yet deep, was substituted.

line-pin, *s.*

Bricklaying: A pin used by bricklayers to hold the line by which the bricks are laid. Its pointed end is forced into a mortar-joint of the building.

line-rocket, *s.*

Pyrotech.: A small rocket made to run along an extended wire or line.

line-winder, *s.* A reel for a clothes-line, a chalk-line, a log-line, &c.

line-wire, *s.*

Teleg.: The wire connecting stations. They are usually of iron, on account of its comparative cheapness and its tenacity, which allows a long reach between posts.

line (2), ***lin**, ***lyne** (2), *s.* [A. S. *lin*, from Latin *linum*=flax.] [LINEN.]

*1. *Ord. Lang.:* Flax, linen.

2. *Fiber:* The finer and longer stapled flax separated from the shorter tow by means of the hackle (q. v.).

line, *v. t.* [LINE (1) & (2), *s.*]

1. To draw lines on or upon; to mark with lines or fine strokes.

2. To draw, to delineate.

"All the pictures fairest *lined*
Are but black to Rosalind."
Shakesp.: As You Like It, iii. 2.

3. To read or repeat line by line.

4. To measure, as land, with a line.

5. To range in a line; as, to *line* soldiers.

¶ In the preceding senses from *line* (1), s.

bôil, bôy; pôut, jôwl; cat, çell, chorus, çhin, bençh; go, ġem; thin, ṭhis; sin, aş; expect, Xenophon, exist. ph = f.
-cian, -tian = shan. -tion, -sion = shŭn; -ṭion, -şion = zhŭn. -tious, -cious, -sious = shŭs. -ble, -dle, &c. = bel, del.

truth

loving now

art or or love

broke and torn

wing

why reach

?

or vow

honest faith is lost

or or deep deep

love constancy

light eyes blind

Or against the thing they see

or or air

against the rut

Stephen Ratcliffe — SONNET 153

Cupid   asleep
Dian   found
his love-
cold valley-fountain   that
from this   fire of Love
heat,   still
grew   which yet
Against
my   eye
would touch my
I   desired
her hied
for
fire

Macgregor Card

SONNET 154

The little Love-god passed out
and put his gun down
accidentally.

There are so many sexes
walking drunkenly this way
or that one.

Don't apologize for being young
inside a house of commerce
notice what your agitations risk
efficiency at any tone
and thank you
for one empty carton of punk hay
after another
how do you say
/EEEEEEEEEEEEEEEEEEEEEE/ in labrador
or strong provincial gallery
in yugo-scotia

Made in the shade
Late in the day

Young in the wood
Laid in the bed
Dead in the shade

Play me a tune
Lay in the water
Dead in the water

Show me your room
Laid in the timber
  Made in the shade
  Dead in the wood
Young in the wood

Show me a tune
Made in the future

Show me a future
Tool in the shed

Young in the future
Long in the shade
Never to shiver
Long in the shade
Made in the wood
Dead in the timber

Show me a tune
    Gallery timbers!

Shiver me
Gallery timbers!

Tree bee bear   Dog bee dog
Tree bear kid   Kid dog ear

Dog *bee* dog
Bee *bee* bee
Bee *dog* bee
Dog *dog* dog

Tree bear bee
Bee dog kid
Kid dog ear
Ear bear bee

Dog bee dog
Ear bee ear
Bee bee bee
Tree *tree* tree

Kid kid dog
Kid kid ear
Kid kid bee
Kid *tree* tree

Dog dog kid
Ear dog kid
Bee dog kid
Tree *tree* kid

beeeeeeeeeeeeeee
doooooooooooog

A beeeeeeeeeeeee
dooooooooooog

A beeeeeeeee
doooooooooooog

A beeeeeeeee
A dooooooog

A A A beeeeeeeeeeeeeeee
A A A doooooooooooog
beeeeeeeeeeeeeeeeeeeeee
doooooooooooooooooog

beeeeeeeeeeee
dooooooog

beee eeeeeeeeeeeeeeeee
doooog
beeeeeeeee
dog

beeee

Index of First Lines

Acknowledgments

Page 1

"Two Alternative Translations of Shakespeare's Sonnet 1: 'From fairest creatures we desire increase'" first appeared in "TRG Research Report 1: Translation" in *Open Letter,* second series, no. 4 (Spring 1973). Copyright © 1973 by Steve McCaffery. Used with permission of the author.

Page 2

"2" from *Nets*, published by Ugly Duckling Presse. Copyright © 2004 by Jen Bervin. Used with permission of the author.

Page 187

"Shakespeare's 116th Sonnet in Black English Translation" from *The Collected Poems of June Jordan*, published by Copper Canyon Press. Copyright © 2005 by The June M. Jordan Literary Trust. Used with permission of the estate.

Page 204

"Dim Lady" from *Sleeping With the Dictionary*, published by University of California Press. Copyright © 2002 by Harryette Mullen. Used with permission of the publisher.

Thanks to Telephone Books managing editor Lauren Hunter for her invaluable help.
Cover image: Adapted from title page of *Shake-speares Sonnets. Neuer before Imprinted.* London: G. Eld T.T. and are to be sold by William Aspley, 1609. Image courtesy of Folger Shakespeare Library.

ISBN: 978-1937658076

Design and typesetting by HR Hegnauer
Text set in Spectrum

Cataloging-in-publication data is available
From the Library of Congress

Distributed by University Press of New England
One Court Street
Lebanon, NH 03766
www.upne.com

Published by Telephone Books, an imprint of Nightboat Books.

Telephone Books
www.distranslation.com

Nightboat Books
www.nightboat.org

Telephone Books / Nightboat Books

Telephone Books, an imprint of Nightboat Books, publishes works of radical translation. For more information about our titles, please visit www.distranslation.com.

Nightboat Books, a nonprofit organization, seeks to develop audiences for writers whose work resists convention and transcends boundaries. We publish books rich with poignancy, intelligence, and risk. Please visit our website, www.nightboat.org, to learn about our titles and how you can support our future publications.

The following individuals have supported the publication of this book. We thank them for their generosity and commitment to the mission of Nightboat Books:

Kazim Ali
Elizabeth Motika
Benjamin Taylor

This book has been made possible, in part, by a grant from the New York State Council on the Arts Literature Program.